RAMBLI
BRADFORD

Volume 1

20 CIRCULAR WALKS IN THE BRADFORD METROPOLITAN DISTRICT

by

Douglas Cossar

for the Ramblers' Association (West Riding Area)

Other publications by the Ramblers' Association (West Riding Area)

Dales Way Handbook (with the Dales Way Association, annually)
Kiddiwalks (new edition Spring 1995)
Douglas Cossar, *Ramblers' Leeds,* 2nd edition,
Volume 1 East of Leeds (1999)
Douglas Cossar, *The Airedale Way* (1996)
Douglas Cossar, *Ramblers' Wakefield* (1997)
Marje Wilson, *The Brontë Way* (1997)

Ramblers' Bradford Volume 1 first published 1999

RAMBLERS' ASSOCIATION (WEST RIDING AREA)
27 Cookridge Avenue, Leeds LS16 7NA

ISBN 1 901184 22 6

Cover photographs
Front: Baildon Bank, Micklethwaite,
Horton Bank Country Park, Thornton Viaduct.
Back: The Doubler Stones, Ilkley Old Bridge, Chellow Dean.

Publishers' Note
At the time of publication all footpaths used in these walks were designated as public rights of way or permissive footpaths, or were paths over which access has traditionally not been denied, but it should be borne in mind that diversion orders may be made or permissions removed. Although every care has been taken in the preparation of this guide, neither the author nor the publisher can accept responsibility for those who stray from the routes described.

this book is affectionately dedicated to

Tom Wilcock

for many years Ramblers' Association
West Riding Area Footpath Secretary and
Chairman of the Bradford Group

who campaigned tirelessly to protect
the footpaths of Bradford

The **Ramblers' Association**, a registered charity, is an organisation dedicated to the preservation and care of the countryside and its network of footpaths, and to helping people to appreciate and enjoy them.

Through its Central Office the Ramblers' Association lobbies and campaigns for more effective legislation to achieve

- the preservation and improvement of the footpath network
- better access to the countryside
- the preservation and enhancement for the benefit of the public of the beauty of the countryside.

Since its formation in 1935 the Ramblers' Association has grown into a powerful campaigning organisation with a membership of 125,000.

The Association relies on many volunteers working at Area and Local Group level to help achieve these objectives.

The **West Riding Area** is one of the 51 Areas of the Ramblers' Association which cover England, Wales and Scotland. It includes the whole of West Yorkshire and parts of North Yorkshire around Selby, York, Harrogate, Ripon, Skipton and Settle, as well as the southern part of the Yorkshire Dales National Park. The Area has over 4,000 members and is divided into 13 Local Groups.

The **Local Groups** carry out the work of the Ramblers' Association by keeping an eye on the state of footpaths in their area and monitoring proposed closures and diversions.

- They put pressure on their Local Authority to take action to remove obstructions and re-instate footpaths after ploughing.
- They do practical work of footpath clearance and waymarking, and can erect stiles and footbridges.
- Where the Local Authority has set up consultation procedures, e.g. Footpath Forums, the Local Group will normally send a representative.
- Many Local Groups produce their own programme of walks.

Regular walks are a very important part of Ramblers' activities. As well as ensuring that local footpaths are used, they provide healthy recreation and the opportunity to make new friends.

If you use and enjoy the footpath network, please help us to protect it, by joining the Ramblers' Association. For further information write to the West Riding Area Membership Secretary

Mrs Dora Tattersall, 2 Southend, Raines Road, Giggleswick, Settle BD24 0BW, or to

The Ramblers' Association, 1/5 Wandsworth Road, London SW8 2XX.

Contents

Walk 1. A Brontë Walk: Ponden Hall, Ponden Kirk
"Wuthering Heights" and the Brontë Falls 9

2. Dean Beck and Keighley Moor 12

3. Silsden to Windgate Nick and the Doubler Stones 15

4. Silsden Moor 18

5. The Swastika Stone, Addingham Moorside and the Dales Way . . .22

6. Austby and Middleton Woods 27

7. Burley in Wharfedale to Burley Moor 29

8. Over Rombald's Moor to Dick Hudson's 31

9. East and West Morton, Sunny Dale and Micklethwaite 35

10. Around Baildon Moor 40

11. Druid's Altar, St.Ives, Harden and Marley 43

12. Harden Moor and the Worth Way .47

13. Old lanes around Oxenhope 52

14. Thornton Moor 55

15. Wilsden to Hewenden and Wood Nook 58

16. Chellow Dean 61

17. Northcliffe Woods, 'Six Days Only' and Heaton Woods 63

18. Thornton to Mountain 65

19. Horton Bank, Clayton and Little Moor 69

20. Royds Hall & Judy Woods 73

Author's note

The Bradford Metropolitan District has much to offer the walker, with considerable landscape variety and a dense network of rights of way. The Aire, with its tributary the Worth, is the only major river, although the Wharfe forms part of the northern boundary, but a myriad of becks flow through steep sided cloughs, and paths contouring high along their sides provide dramatic views. The area is hilly almost everywhere, and long vistas open up when one is least expecting them. One of the most spectacular is from Horton Bank Top (Walk 19), not far from the centre of the city. Another is from Top Withens (Walk 1), high on the heather moorland in the west.

Bradford's rise to a large manufacturing city took place in the 19th century, and there are many remains of its industrial heritage: mills with their high chimneys, mill reservoirs, railways with spectacular viaducts, often now sadly abandoned, abound, and of course through the Aire valley passes the Leeds and Liverpool Canal, with its associated warehouses, bridges, locks, including the famous Bingley Three and Five Rise (Walk 9) and housing. The towpath is a fascinating and often very attractive source of level walking.

But relics of Bradford's pre-industrial heritage are also plentiful. Among the oldest are the prehistoric carvings and stone circles on Ilkley Moor (Walks 5 and 8), but I particularly enjoy the old farmhouses, often dating back to the 17th century, many of them now well-restored as modern "desirable residences", the causeyed paths used by the traders and the quarrymen of old, and the stone packhorse bridges. And no rambler hereabouts will want to ignore the heritage of the Brontës, the local scenery and buildings which played such a great role in their lives and works.

Almost all the walks are entirely within the Bradford Metropolitan District, although I have allowed myself to stray over the border from time to time for the sake of a more interesting ramble. I have tried to achieve a wide geographical spread of walks, and I hope that *Ramblers' Bradford* represents reasonably well the variety and interest of the landscapes of Bradford.

All the paths used are definitive rights of way or permissive footpaths, or occasionally paths where no one is likely to object to your using them. The ones used in this book are on the whole in good shape, although some can become overgrown in the summer and muddy after wet weather. If you should encounter any obstacles, obstructions, nuisances or other difficulties, please report them, to Bradford Council's Public Rights of Way Section, Holycroft, Goulbourne Street, Keighley BD21 1PY (tel. 01535-618300). As a result of recent tragic accidents, dogs now seem generally to be kept under much better control than formerly, but there are still some irresponsible owners, and do look out for bulls at large in pastures in the summer months, and take suitable evasive action, even if this means a minor trespass. Better safe than sorry!

All the walks can be located on the Ordnance Survey Landranger map 104 (Leeds & Bradford, Harrogate & Ilkley) except for parts of Walks 1 and 2, which spill over onto Sheet 103 (Blackburn & Burnley), and at the start of each walk I have given details of the relevant Pathfinder/Explorer/Outdoor Leisure sheet(s). The new Explorer map for Bradford & Huddersfield to be published in September 1999 will replace some of the Pathfinder sheets. The sketch maps which accompany each walk are based upon Ordnance Survey 1:25 000 scale mapping with the permission of the Controller of Her Majesty's Stationery Office © Crown copyright; Licence no: 43323U. They are intended to give an overview of the walk and to supplement the description, but as they are greatly simplified, particularly in built-up areas, **they should not be used as a substitute for the description**. Please read the descriptions carefully: I have tried to make them clear and unambiguous and to eliminate the risk of misinterpretation. I am sure you will let me know where I have failed! But in my experience lots of people go astray through not concentrating on the text of a walk, inadvertently skipping a line or jumping by mistake from one stile to the next, or just losing the place through being engrossed in conversation with their companions!

Almost all the walks are accessible by public transport, and I have given details as they are known to me at the moment. But please do check this information with West Yorkshire Metro (Tel: 0113-245-7676).

As you do the walks, you will come across references to long-distance footpaths, which for at least part of their length are within the Bradford District. The following are the main ones. The **Pennine Way**, the first and best known of the National Trails, 250 miles from Derbyshire to the Scottish Borders, is in the Bradford District for only a mile or two, as it crosses Stanbury Moor and Oakworth Moor, but it is met with on Walk 1. The **Dales Way**, 81 miles from Ilkley to Bowness on Windermere, is encountered on Walk 5, and the Bradford-Ilkley Dales Way Link on Walk 8. The **Airedale Way** is a 50-mile route from Leeds City Station to Malham Tarn, which follows as far as possible riverside paths. Part of Walk 11 uses its route. The **Brontë Way** stretches for 40 miles from Oakwell Hall, Birstall to Gawthorpe Hall in Padiham and visits many places associated with the lives and works of the Brontë family. We meet it briefly on Walks 13, 18 and 19. The West Riding Area of the Ramblers' Association publishes guidebooks to both the Airedale and the Brontë Ways, which are widely available in local bookshops and TICs.

There are so many good walks in the Bradford District that I have decided to make this Volume 1 of two. If you enjoy the rambles in this book, do look out for Volume 2, which I hope will appear early in 2000.

Happy walking!

Douglas Cossar
August 1999

The location of the walks

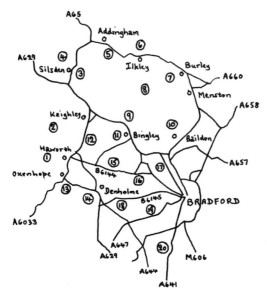

Acknowledgements

I am most grateful to the staff of the Bradford Metropolitan District Rights of Way Section for giving me their time and the benefit of their knowledge of local footpath developments and for suggesting corrections and improvements to my routes. The final responsibility for the walks is of course my own. My thanks also to David Parsons of the Bradford Countryside Service for permission to use his photographs of Ponden Hall (Walk 1), Ilkley Manor House (Walk 5), White Wells (Walk 8) and the plaque on the wall of the Brontë birthplace in Thornton (Walk 18). Joyce Broughton helped me with her knowledge of local paths around Clayton.

It is a great pleasure to me to dedicate this small volume to Tom Wilcock. My first job after joining the Ramblers' Association was to be Secretary of the West Riding Area Footpaths Committee, of which Tom was Chairman. He was also Area Footpaths Officer. He immediately made a great impression on me, not only because of his astonishing knowledge of West Riding footpaths and the time he spent looking into diversion proposals, reports of obstructions, and so on, but also because of the gentleness, firmness, tact, courtesy and diplomacy he brought to all his dealings with stroppy ramblers and farmers alike. He is a real gentleman, and over the years I came to have very great respect and affection for him. All those who use public footpaths in the West Riding area owe him an immense debt of gratitude, and I should like on their behalf to say Thank you to him and wish him well for the future.

A BRONTË WALK: PONDEN HALL, PONDEN KIRK, "WUTHERING HEIGHTS" AND THE BRONTË FALLS

WALK 1

6 miles (9½ km); Outdoor Leisure 21. A moderately strenuous walk, because of two stiff ascents, but worth every breath. Sweeping views and fine moorland scenery. Sections of Pennine Way and Brontë Way. This is almost certainly the countryside which was in Emily Brontë's mind when she wrote her "Wuthering Heights", and she must have rearranged bits and pieces of landscape and buildings which were familiar to her to create the new reality of her novel. Certainly Ponden Hall and Top Withens, traditionally the models for Thruscross Grange and Wuthering Heights, are very different from the houses described in the novel. There is even a local tradition that the original "Brontë waterfall" was the one below Ponden Kirk, which we pass on this walk, rather than the more famous one, which we also visit. But historical puzzles and uncertainties cannot detract from the quality of the scenery and the pleasures of walking through it.

At the far end of the village of Stanbury coming from Haworth a tarmac lane forks off left and there is room to park a few cars. This is also the terminus of the 664 hourly bus from Keighley (not evenings or Sundays). The walk starts here. For additional parking drive up the tarmac lane, ignore one forking right, and just after the tarmac ends the lane widens and there is plenty of room to park.

Walk up the lane, keep right at the first fork and on reaching Buckley Green fork right on the unsurfaced track (here joining both the Pennine Way and the Brontë Way) and follow it to the next house. Just before the tarmac starts, cross the stile on the right and walk downhill to the next tarmac lane, and turn left along the side of Ponden Reservoir. The road bends right and climbs, then turns left past Ponden Hall.

Continue along the track and about 150 yards past the Hall fork left up a concrete farm access road, here leaving the Pennine and Brontë Ways. The track climbs past a farm entrance to a gate leading onto the open moor. Continue by the wall on the right, but 80 yards after it turns sharp right fork left off the track (by a signpost) and walking at right angles to your previous line follow the path to the next wall ahead. There turn right and follow this wall up. Where the wall turns left and drops into Ponden Clough, keep forward on a good path which contours round the head of the valley.

Ponden Hall

Cross the beck at the top over stone slabs near a small waterfall and continue on the path as it contours round the edge of the clough. When you reach a cluster of ruins on the right, the outcrop of rocks on the left is Ponden Kirk. The path leads down to cross another beck by means of large rocks (ignore a steep path with a handrail leading down into the clough from here), then climbs along the edge on the other side. Eventually the clear path descends gently towards a wall. Keep this on your left and follow it to Far Slack Farm.

Just before the ladder-stile at the farm turn right and take the clear path following the fence on your left uphill. There is no right of way for about 100 yards, but no one is likely to object. When the fence becomes a wall, you are back on a public footpath. At the top turn right along the track (Pennine Way again) and follow it all the way to Top Withins. Shortly before you reach it the track narrows to a paved footpath, and by the ruins of a farm on the right a clear path descends left into the valley (signpost). That will be your onward route.

So after visiting Top Withins, return to this point and take the path downhill. Soon you have a beck on your right and the paved path descends to cross by stepping stones another beck coming in from the left. About 100 yards after this ignore a path forking right, and follow the clear path ahead until having crossed various stiles you cross the remains of a stile in a broken wall. A few yards further on fork right on the descending path which soon becomes paved and leads to a kissing-gate, from which there is a good view of the Brontë Falls across the valley. Go down to have a closer look at the falls, the bridge and the "Brontë Chair" if you wish, but then return to this gate.

With your back to the gate and looking uphill, take the path forking right up to the next signpost (Brontë Way again). Bear right for a few yards along a section of old walled lane, then turn left to the next signpost, then half right over the field to a ladder-stile. Now walk forward with the remains of a wall on the right to the next signpost. Here leave the Brontë Way and keep straight forward to a wall corner, where you kink through left and then right and continue forward with a wall on your right.

When the wall turns sharp right, keep straight forward to a gate with a kissing-gate beside it. Keep on along the track, in a few yards ignoring a minor track forking left, and on reaching a junction of tracks, bear right through the small gate beside the cattle-grid and follow the track back to the start. The defensive position of Stanbury, the "fortification on stony ground" on a ridge between two valleys is well seen. The reservoir is Lower Laithe.

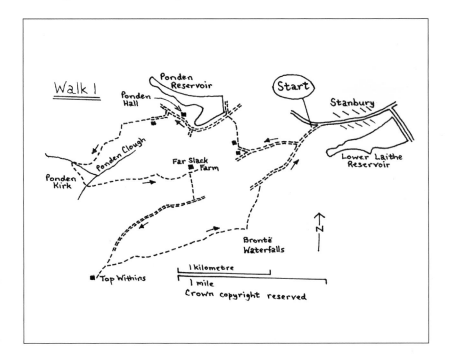

DEAN BECK AND KEIGHLEY MOOR

WALK 2

5¾ miles (9¼ km); Outdoor Leisure 21. A very fine ramble, contrasting the gentle beauty of the valley of Dean Beck with the upland solitude of Keighley Moor. One of the best in the book! Close attention must be paid to route finding on one section.

The walk starts at Hare Hill Edge picnic site, on the road from Oakworth to Laneshaw Bridge, 350 yards west of the Grouse Inn (GR 007 384), marked by a large layby and a couple of picnic tables. Do try to fit in a visit to the Grouse Inn, a lovely old Timothy Taylor pub of great charm. There is no convenient public transport.

Walk along the road towards Oakworth for about 200 yards, then take the signposted footpath through a stile by a gate on the left and walk uphill with a wall on the right. Pass through a few yards of walled lane and keep on by the wall on the right. Pass through an old gateway in a broken wall and in 30 yards cross a step-stile in the wall on the right and turn left, keeping by the wall. About 50 yards before the end of the field bear half right across it to a gap-stile in the wall ahead. Go through, and follow a high wall on your right. Where this ends, cross the ladder-stile by the gate on the right and turn left along the walled lane. When the wall on the left ends, keep on by the wall on the right.

Go through a gate - Nook Farm is to the right - and keep forward along the lane, which is now surfaced. On reaching a T-junction, turn right, pass Broad Head Farm and follow the road to the next junction. Cross straight over into the track opposite. Soon Newsholme village appears half right. When the track bends right towards it, turn left along another track which leads to a stile by a gate. Follow the path straight downhill into the valley ahead. This is the wooded Cat Clough, which leads down to Newsholme Dean. Having crossed the beck near the foot, keep on down the slope. At the foot go through the gate and cross Dean Beck by either the clapper bridge or the packhorse bridge beside it. Follow the wall on the right, which soon bends right to reach two gates. Go through the left hand one and walk up by the wall on the right.

At the top of the field go through the gateway ahead and keep on up on a path which soon bends right. Follow the wall on the right up until you reach a clear cross track and turn left up this. The track curves left and crosses a small beck, and now take the right fork, on an ascending grassy track. Glorious views open up over the valley. After a time the track has the remains of causey stones. Follow it up to a road and turn left along this. After 40 yards fork left down the access road to Bottoms Farm. Now you must pay close attention to route finding! At the entrance to the farm fork right off the concrete drive up the grass to pass a bench and go through a small gate, then continue by the wall on the left. Pass to the right of a barn to a stile in the wall corner.

Bear left then right to cross a small beck on the stones of an old wall. Now turn left on a clear path which passes to the left of a birch tree and climbs gently up the slope with a deep ravine down to the left. It soon bears right away from the ravine along the top of a small grassy bank and passes through an old gateway in a broken wall. Pass round to the right of the small hillock in front of you and you will see a footpath sign ahead. From it bear slightly left to a large gate in the next facing wall. Cross the step-stile beside it and walk straight across the next field to the stile in the wall opposite, then straight over the next field to the next stile, then straight over the next one, making for the wall on the left.

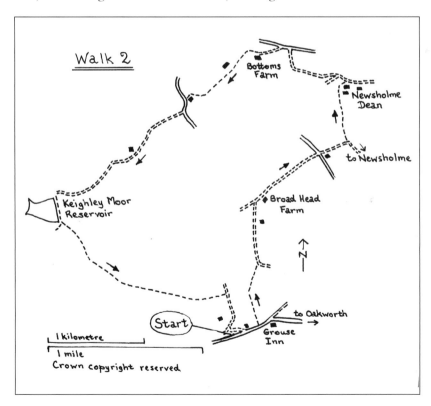

Follow this for a short distance, and when over the brow of the hill head for a gateway. Go through and follow the power line poles down the next field.

Finally drop steeply to where Dean Beck is joined by another beck coming from the right. Ford this smaller beck and go through the gate opposite. Keep forward with the beck to your left. Across the beck you will soon notice a wall coming down the hillside. When you draw level with it, the right of way turns half right up the field to the farm, but the farmer prefers you to continue along the bottom of the field to the next corner, there turning right uphill with the wall on your left. Go through a large gate on the left and walk through the yard of Slitheroford Farm to the road. Turn left downhill to Morkin Bridge, where there is a large layby. From the layby cross the stile beside the large metal gate and follow the narrow tarmac road all the way up to Keighley Moor Reservoir. You are now in a large area of urban common which you can explore at will.

Cross the reservoir dam then keep forward to a fork at a concrete pillar. Fork left along a grassy track over the moor. A little way along, at what looks like another fork, keep left. The track soon narrows to a clear footpath, which can be wet in places, which will lead you without fail to a wall corner where there is a boundary stone. Keep on with the wall on your left, parallel to a row of shooting butts on the right. When you reach an old gateway in the wall, go through and turn right, now keeping the wall on your right. The path here is much less clear. Stay by the wall until you reach a cross wall. Cross the stile in the corner and continue forward, keeping to the left of a broken wall.

On reaching the next cross wall, turn right up a track. Pass through a gate and bear left with the track to another gate, being joined by another track coming from Harehill House on the right. Go through the gate, bear right and follow the track as it winds down towards the road. On the last sharp left hand bend, where a minor track forks down to the right, leave the track and take the path to the right of the telegraph pole, which drops steeply directly to the picnic site from which you started.

SILSDEN TO WINDGATE NICK AND THE DOUBLER STONES

WALK 3

5½ miles (9 km); Outdoor Leisure 21. Field paths and tracks, a wooded ghyll with waterfalls, fine views of Airedale and Wharfedale. A short stiff climb up to Windgate Nick.

The walk starts at the War Memorial in the centre of Silsden. Silsden is served by buses 70/80 Skipton-Keighley, 713 Keighley-Silsden (hourly), 712/762/765 Ilkley-Keighley (hourly). The Wesley Place car park close to the start is Pay & Display, but by driving up the main road and turning right along Dale View free on-street parking is available (in this case start the walk at [*]).

Go to the street at the back of the War Memorial and turn right. Just past the Catholic Church and before the Methodist Church turn left and cross the footbridge into the park. Go left at the first fork, i.e. not up the steps on the right; you are soon joined by a path from the right. Having passed the tennis courts take the right fork and keep the courts on your right. Cross straight over the next broad drive, up three steps, now with houses on the left, up a few more steps, turn right at the street and at the next corner left up Fletcher Avenue. At the next junction turn right (this is Dale View), [*] walk along with the playing fields on your right and turn left up Banklands Avenue, then first right along Hawber Cote Drive.

Cross the stile at the end of the street, walk forward for a few yards to pass through a gateway and bear left to follow the hedge on your left. Pass through a kissing-gate and continue up the wall/hedge to the top. Ignore the stile ahead onto the road and turn left over another stile, then follow the wall on your right. Go through the kissing-gate in the next corner and continue by the wall. In the next corner ignore the stile ahead and go through the gap-stile on the right and walk up the walled path. Cross the stile at the end and keep on by the wall on your left. Pass to the right of the house at the top and keep forward down its access drive to a road. Cross over and take the farm access road opposite.

Walk straight through the yard at the farm, pass through the large wooden gate at the far end and continue up the stony track. About 30 yards before this reaches two gates in a corner turn right off it and walk up the grass to what looks like the start of a walled lane. Cross the stile by the gate and walk down the right hand edge of the field. Cross the stile at the bottom and keep on down to cross the beck. Walk straight up the next large field, aiming for the large farm of North End. You skirt round to the left of some broken ground and head for a gap-stile clearly visible in the wall ahead, a few yards to the left of a gate. Keep your line up to the next stile, then up the next field to a stile in the wall corner between the farmhouse on the left and an outbuilding on the right.

Bear slightly right along the front of the house to the next stile by a gate, then bear right up the slope to pass through a large metal gate, then left to the wall ahead, and follow this wall on your right up to the top corner. Ignore the stile ahead and turn left with the wall, then follow it up to the next road. Turn left and enjoy the views left over Airedale. Shortly after the road levels out a footpath sign points right over a stile. Cross this and climb steeply with the wall on your right. After the gradient eases, there is a wood over the wall. After a time there is a fine view over Wharfedale. At the far end of the wood cross the stile on the right and start climbing again, with another wall on your right. Pass through the cleft of Windgate Nick and cross the stile straight ahead in the corner.

Now the Doubler Stones are visible ahead. Follow the path which leads most directly to them. Shortly before reaching them you pass through a kissing-gate in a fence. Climb to the stones, then drop down the slope to the farm below. Follow the track into the farmyard and bear left with it to pass to the right of the farmhouse. Leave the farm by the gate at the far end and walk straight down the field to the next gate beside a very large rock. Now continue down the track with a wall on your right. Follow the wall down to a gap-stile by a gate, pass through and turn right to keep following the wall. At a cattle-grid you join a track. Follow this to the next farm, Ghyll Grange.

Pass through the farmyard, in which the track makes a sharp turn right, then another one left. Having left the farm, take the first track on the left, which leads to a gate. A track now bears left round the outside of the farm buildings to a double gate. Pass through and turn right down another track. Go through the next gate into a large field and immediately turn right to follow the wall on the right down until you reach a clear track curving left (there is a stile in the wall on the right at this point). Follow the track down and cross the footbridge just to the right of the huge water pipe, then bear right to rejoin the track. Go through the gate, but a few yards further on when the track curves left, keep straight on along a clear footpath, with Holden Beck down below on the right.

After you cross the next stile the path descends a little to cross a side beck by a massive stepping stone then continues beside the wall on the left. A little further along look out for a fork, where you must keep right on the descending path. If you wish to view two waterfalls, take the steps dropping steeply on the right with a handrail, but the walk keeps forward on the clear path through woodland, now contouring, now dropping gently, now climbing slightly. Shortly after leaving the wood you join a track which leads to a road. Keep forward steeply down this.

At the foot pass the entrance to Howden Park Farms on the left, cross the beck and in a few yards fork right off the road up to a gate. Bear slightly right up the field, aiming for the first power line pole, then keep that line to find a stile in a stretch of wall near the top corner. Continue in the same direction over the corner of the next field to another stile, then bear left along the fence on your left to the next stile out onto the Tomling Cote access road. Walk forward along this, but where it bends left keep forward to a stile onto Silsden golf course. Walk along by the hedge on your left. After a short stretch with trees on both sides bear left to pass to the left of a solitary tree, then continue your previous line with a strip of rough ground then another row of trees on your right. When you reach a small wood, keep to the right of it, then along to the left of another line of trees. Follow the trees until you pass the smooth turf of the 13th tee on the left, then turn left and cross the rough grass to a stile in the wall, near where this becomes a hedge. (This path may be diverted because of golf course developments: look out for waymarks.) Bear half right down the field to a stile by a gate (ignoring a stile in the wall on the left), then turn left down the road and follow it through Brunthwaite.

At the road junction turn right up Hawber Lane, then enter the yard of Drabble House Farm on the left. Cross the yard and go through the gate then bear left down the side of the farmhouse. Cross the stile in the bottom corner and follow the wall on your left down to the end of the next field, where you go through the gap in the wall just to the left of the gate (ignoring the gap in the wall on the left). Walk along the street, turn left at the next junction, then immediately right along Craven Drive. At the foot of the hill, where the road turns left, go down the ginnel on the right. On reaching the playing fields turn left and follow the surfaced path, then a lane, back to the centre of Silsden.

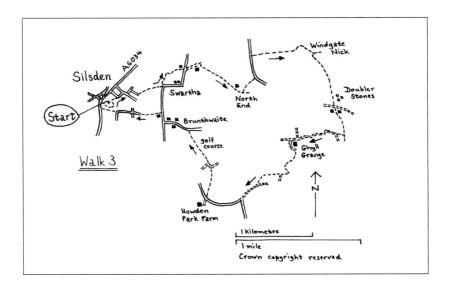

17

SILSDEN MOOR

WALK 4

7¼ miles (11½ km); Outdoor Leisure 21. Easy walking in upland pastoral countryside with many fine old farmhouses.

The walk starts at the War Memorial in the centre of Silsden. Silsden is served by buses 70/80 Skipton-Keighley, 713 Keighley-Silsden (hourly), 712/762/765 Ilkley-Keighley (hourly). The Wesley Place car park close to the start is Pay & Display, but by driving up the main road and turning right along Dale View free on-street parking is available. There are toilets on the other side of the main road from the War Memorial.

From the War Memorial bear right round the rose bed, cross the main road, turn right for a few yards, then left along Bell Square. After a few yards turn right, between the Kings Arms and its car park, bear right over the bridge and continue up Chapel Street, which becomes North Street. After a time the road narrows and soon begins to bend right. Fork left up Breakmoor Avenue and in a few yards fork left again. Immediately you are faced by a fork: keep right, but when this un-made-up road bends right, keep straight forward down a ginnel.

Cross the stile at the end and walk diagonally right down the field. Soon a footbridge appears, which you cross, then turn right to a stile and continue parallel to the beck to the next stile. Now bear slightly left uphill away from the beck, diagonally up the field. Pass close to the corner of a wood then keep your line towards a large gate by the next wood corner. Cross the stile by the gate and follow the track. At the end cross the stile in the wall ahead, then bear left to follow the hedge on the left towards Hay Hills Farm. A few yards before the farm cross a sleeper bridge and stile on the left and turn right to follow the boundary fence of the farm. Cross the wall ahead in the field corner, jump the ditch and turn right to the farm.

Cross the stile by the gate ahead and cross diagonally left over two farm tracks to the next stile. Cross the next field diagonally to the far corner. Cross the stile and follow the right hand edge of the field with a beck down on your right. About 15 yards before the next field corner cross the stile on the right, then a footbridge and another stile, and follow the hedge on your left along to the next stile. Pass to the left of Ivy House and follow the access road up to the next motor road, passing another farm on the way. Turn right at the road, but a few yards after the entrance into a bungalow called Romille and opposite the access road to Dalesbank Holiday Park cross the stile in the wall on the left and walk along the left hand edge of the field, past the bungalow.

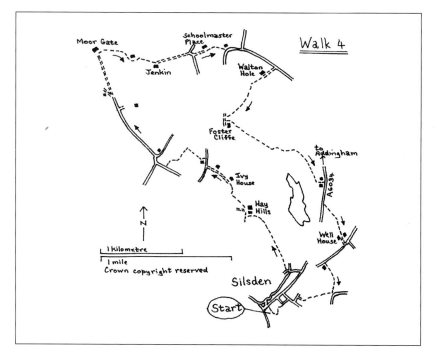

In the next corner turn right with the fence/hedge, and in the next corner cross the stile and immediately turn left over a sleeper bridge and another stile, then walk forward along the right hand edge of the field. Pass through a gateway and continue along the edge of the next field to a stile by a gate onto Horn Lane. Turn right. At the next T-junction turn right again, and at the next fork keep left up Kiln Hill Lane. Follow this road until it forks, with both branches crossing cattle-grids. Keep right along the private road to Moorgate Farm. There is a fine view left over Airedale. Immediately before the farm turn right along the track, passing farm buildings, and at the end of these leave the track and keep forward with a wall on your left to a gate in the field corner. Go through and walk straight down the next long field to another gate at the far end, then continue with a wall on your left.

Pass round to the right of Crow Trees Farm, follow the track through the gate ahead and continue along it with a wall on your left. Follow the track through another gate, pass to the left of Jenkin Farm and stay on the track all the way to the next road. Turn right for a yard or two, then take the next farm access road on the left. Walk straight past the farmhouse at Schoolmaster Place, go through the gate at the far end of the yard and continue along the track. Now beware! About 15 yards

19

before the track goes through another gate, fork left off it to cross a stile in the wall on the left. Cross the next field at an angle of about 35° to the wall you have just crossed, to a stile out onto the next road.

Turn left along the road. Ignore Jowett's Lane and follow Cringles Lane until you reach a walled lane on the right entered by a ladder-stile beside a gate. Walk down this, passing the derelict Walton Hole, dated 1719, pass through the gate at the far end of the yard and drop to cross Cowburn Beck by a footbridge. Walk straight forward up the other side (a nice spot for a picnic), climb the bank and bear slightly left to the hedge over on the left. Follow it for a yard or two, but when it turns left, keep straight forward along a bank marking an old field boundary to a gate. Go through and follow the right hand edge of the next field. A few yards before the far corner of this field cross a stile in the wall on the right and turn left, now following the wall/fence on your left. You join a track which comes through a gate on the left: keep forward to a gate ahead and turn left down the tarmac lane.

Cross a squeeze-stile by a large white gate, then immediately before the gate into the grounds of the house ahead go through a small gate on the left and turn right to walk along the field to the next small gate ahead. Walk down the right hand edge of the next field for 50 yards to yet another small metal gate in the wall on the right. Go through and bear half left to walk down the right hand edge of the next field. Soon Foster Cliff Beck is below you on the right. Follow the fence all the way to the bottom of the field, where a footpath descends steeply through the trees to beck level. Cross the stile and turn left, but ignore a ford leading to a clear path up the bank on the other side of the beck, keeping the beck on your right, and ford it just before it flows into Great Gill Beck on the left. Now keeping the beck on your left you reach a footbridge.

Cross the bridge, climb the few steps and walk along with the beck on your right for about 20 yards, then climb steeply up the bank on your left through the hawthorn trees - there is no clear path - bearing left to a fence at the top. Keep this fence on your left. Cross the stile in the next facing wall and continue by the fence/wall on your left, crossing over a track on the way, then ignoring a ladder-stile, crossing another wall by a stile (Silsden Reservoir is now half right). Cross another stile and now you are in an enclosed path. Cross the stile at the end and turn left up the track to the main road, using the high stile on the left of the metal gate ahead. Turn right down the footway. You could follow the main road all the way back to Silsden, but this is rather boring. So opposite the entrance into Fishbeck on the right, cross the stile by the gate on the other side of the road (immediately after a walled layby) and walk half right to the top corner of the large field. Cross the stile and bear left up a short section of walled lane, then turn right and follow the wall on your right.

About two-thirds of the way along the field bear half left to a small gate by a large telegraph pole. Keep your direction over the next field, to the left hand end of the house, go through a large metal gate onto a tarmac drive and pass between the two dwelling-houses at Well House, then follow the drive to the next road. Turn right. Immediately before the next farm on the left, Raikes House, cross the stile on the left and follow the wall/fence on your right. Cross the stile in the field corner and turn left, with the wall now on your left, to a gated stile in the next corner. Go through, ignore the gap-stile on the left and walk forward to the iron kissing-gate in the next corner, then continue with the wall on your left to the step-stile.

Cross it, again ignore a stile on the left and turn sharp right down the right hand edge of the field. Go through the iron kissing-gate at the foot and keep on down the edge of the next field. At the foot bear right through a gap in the hedge and a few yards further on cross a stile onto a street. Walk forward along this, turn left at the T-junction and right at the next T-junction (with playing fields ahead) then left at the next street (Fletcher Avenue), at the bottom turning right with the road for 20 yards, then take the footpath on the left down a few steps and to the left of a hedge. Go down a few more steps and turn right, then immediately left, pass the tennis courts on your left, and on reaching a fork, keep right, cross the beck by the footbridge and follow the road forward. Turn right with the road and walk along to your starting point.

DID YOU KNOW that you can walk out of Leeds City Station, turn right and in a few minutes find yourself on a direct footpath route to the source of the River Aire, 50 miles away at Malham Tarn in the heart of the Yorkshire Dales?

Details of the whole route, which follows as far as possible riverside paths, are given in Douglas Cossar's *The Airedale Way*.

The book contains 16 circular and 2 linear rambles which cover the whole of Airedale from Malham Tarn to Castleford and include the entire towpath of the Leeds and Liverpool Canal between Leeds and Gargrave. Riverside paths and walks to notable viewpoints open up a variety of landscapes and a wealth of natural beauty, with old stone bridges, ancient churches, picturesque villages, historic farmhouses and many relics of the Industrial Revolution.

The Airedale Way is published by the West Riding Area of the RA at **£4.50** and is available from local booksellers, or direct from the publishers at 27 Cookridge Avenue, Leeds LS16 7NA price £5.50 including post & packing (cheques payable to Ramblers' Association please).

THE SWASTIKA STONE, ADDINGHAM MOORSIDE AND THE DALES WAY

Walk 5

7 miles (11¼ km); Explorer 27. Easy moorland and riverside paths; some delightful field paths which are a pleasant exercise in route-finding; a short section of the Dales Way; glorious views of mid-Wharfedale. Ilkley is one of the jewels in the crown of the Bradford District. Olicana was a Roman fort, and the mediaeval parish church was built on part of its site. A flourishing spa in Victorian times, Ilkley is now a thriving residential town for those who work in Bradford and Leeds. Not to be missed are the Anglo-Saxon crosses in the parish church, the 16th-century Manor House, now a charming museum and the Old Grammar School of 1637 in Addingham Road, now merely a cottage. On the moors around Ilkley are many prehistoric carvings and stone circles, of which the Swastika Stone, an example of a common motif in Celtic art and possibly of Iron Age date, is one of the more famous.

The walk starts at the railway/bus station in Ilkley. Trains and/or buses are available from Bradford, Leeds, Keighley and Skipton. If coming by car, from the traffic lights in the centre of Ilkley drive up Brook Street (signposted Ilkley Moor) and at the top bear left then immediately right up the one-way Wells Road; over the cattle grid at the top there is

Ilkley Manor House

a car park immediately on the right. Park here. Walk to the far end of the car park, go up three steps on the left and follow the clear path. Cross a footbridge and continue ascending, to reach an entrance drive to the former Ilkley College. Now join the walk at [*].

Walk along the front of the old railway station building towards the town centre, cross the main road on your left at the pedestrian crossing, turn right to cross the foot of Wells Road, then at the two telephone kiosks bear slightly left to enter the gardens between the next two streets. Make your way up through the gardens, which have a beck flowing through them, to the top, making sure that you leave the gardens with the beck on your left. Cross Queens Road (the main road ahead of you) and turn right along it for a few yards, then turn left up Linnburn Mews. When the track bends right, take the footpath on the left.

Cross straight over the former Ilkley College access road to the footpath opposite, which in a few yards passes through a kissing-gate. A little further on ignore a footbridge on the left, then another one down some steps, and keep the beck down on your left and the iron fence of the college grounds on your right. On reaching another college entrance drive, [*] cross diagonally left, follow the path by the fence to the road and turn right along it. Pass the White Wells car park on the left and another entrance to Ilkley College on the right.

Where the road forks by the Glenmoor Centre go left, and 60 yards before the road crosses a bridge fork right onto a grassy track, cross a footbridge and continue with a high wall and houses to the right along the edge of the moor. After the houses end you pass a reservoir, then 20 yards before a wooden footbridge over a ghyll and a wood, by a couple of benches, find a clear path ascending half-left which leads across the beck by a plank bridge

The Swastika Stone

about 60 yards upstream from the wooden footbridge. Pass through a gap in an old wall with the upright of an iron gate, and the railings protecting the Swastika Stone can be seen ahead; from it there are fine views from Otley Chevin round to Beamsley Beacon and Addingham.

Continue along the moor edge path. The following are the features you encounter en route (in order): gap-stile, wide walled lane, wall to your right, gap-stile, a few low trees, broken down wall to cross (with a gap-stile a few yards left of the crossing point), gap-stile, ladder-stile, large cairn on left, ladder-stile, (here ignore a path descending on the right)

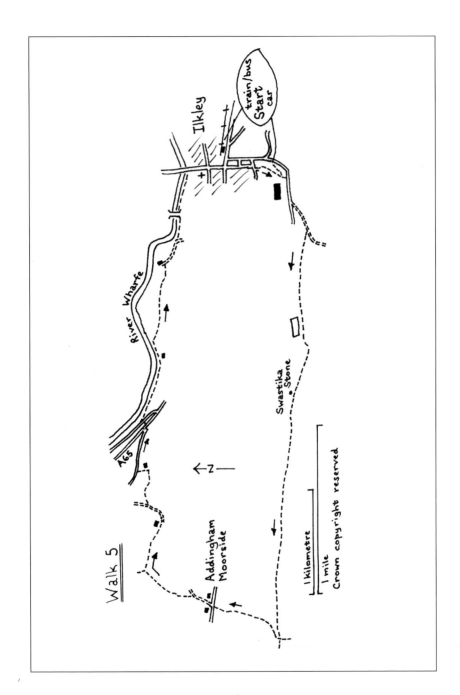

Walk 5

Ilkley

train/bus
Start
car

River Wharfe

Swastika Stone

Addingham Moorside

265

← N —

1 kilometre
1 mile
Crown copyright reserved

24

series of cairns, step-stile, large isolated boulder, two step-stiles, cairned path through heather some yards left of edge of moor, and soon there is a view left to the two mushroom-like Doubler Stones (Walk 3) and to Airedale. When you reach a crossing of paths by a cairn, with a gap-stile in the wall 60 yards to your left, take the path descending on the right.

In a short distance at the foot of the crag take the right fork, which leads down quite gently to a stile in the wall at the bottom. Over it, head straight down the rough pasture (towards the houses) to meet a wall coming from the left and curving downhill: keep this wall on your left and you will reach a stile in it in the bottom corner. Cross this and keep on down, now with the wall on your right, to a stile onto a minor road.

Cross straight over and go down the access road to Stegg House Farm with the beck to your right. Just before the road crosses the beck by a cattle grid bear left along with a fence to your left. In a few yards you reach a gap-stile into a field. Now the route-finding should be fun! Walk straight forward down the slope, soon to pick up a broken wall: keep to the right of it and where it bears left bear left with it, but in a few yards bear right again, down the slope to a step-stile in the cross-wall at the bottom.

Continue down with the wall to your left to the next stile, then straight down across the next field to the next one. Now bear slightly right, to drop to a stile in the bottom right hand corner of the field. Ignore the footbridge on the left and walk straight on over the next stile. The path climbs, keeping close to the edge of the field on the left, then at the top of the rise drops to cross another side beck.

Walk along the middle of the next long field, tending slightly to the left hand side, to pass through a kissing-gate and then keep to the left of a beck which is marked by a line of trees. Follow the left hand edge of the field to pass through a gate and continue forward to a step-stile to the right of another gate just before the next farm. Pass to the right of the house, through a gate, and straight on along the farm access road. At the second cattle grid you are joined by another track from the right.

100 yards further on, before you reach two large old trees, bear half-right off the track and down the slope to the beck. Keep this on your right until you can cross it by a stony ford. Walk forward, then bear right with the fence on your right; the fence becomes a wall and turns left: ignore the gap-stile in it, and follow it along to the farm, turning left again at the end of the field to walk along the rear of the farm and follow the fence on your right to a gate and a road. Now route-finding is easy again!

Turn right along the road. When you reach the A65 cross straight over (care!) to find a path which bears right and winds through the trees to the old road. Cross this and bear left for a few yards then sharp right with the river Wharfe to your left. (You are now on the Dales Way.) Follow the riverside track/path, which can be muddy in places, back to Ilkley.

Be careful at one point to drop down a few steps to cross a footbridge on the left. Just after passing a pumping station you cross another footbridge. Go through a kissing-gate. Follow the fence on your left to another kissing-gate, and now the fence is on your right. Through another (white) kissing-gate bear left, with the fence now to your left, and after the next one follow the fence on your right; through the next one bear right again along the fence on your right, and through the next one slightly left; through the next one bear right along the access road to the Tennis Club.

Where the drive bears right keep straight on along the footpath to the 17th century bridge in Ilkley, the official start of the Dales Way (signpost to Bowness 84 miles!). At the near end of the bridge a stile leads down a few steps to the continuation of the riverside path. Go up the steps to the right of the next bridge onto the road and turn right up the road. At the traffic lights either go right to visit the Parish Church and the Manor House Museum behind it, or cross straight over to return to the station. (Car drivers should then jump to the start of the walk description.)

The start of the Dales Way

AUSTBY AND MIDDLETON WOODS

WALK 6

4 miles (6¼ km); Explorer 27. Riverside and woodland walking (masses of bluebells), with some fine views of Wharfedale. Muddy in the woods after rain.

The walk starts at Ilkley Parish Church. Ilkley can be reached by train or bus from Bradford, Leeds, Keighley and Skipton and there is town centre parking.

From the church walk down New Brook Street, noticing that the church is built on the site of the Roman fort of Olicana, cross the river bridge, built in 1904, and 30 yards further on turn left down some steps and bear right along the riverside. Pass the 17th-century bridge and go through the gate ahead to continue along the riverside path. On reaching the golf course the path moves away from the river and reaches a road. Cross straight over into the street opposite, in a few yards turning left into Owler Park Road. Where the road turns right, fork left over a stile (signposted Nesfield) and follow the path through woodland to a stile into a field.

Walk across the field parallel to the fence on the left, at the far side bearing right along the fence, crossing the beck and a stile, and climbing steeply right through the trees to a stile into another field. Drop to cross a footbridge, from which you bear left and then right to walk across the field parallel to the houses of Low Austby. At the far side of the field ignore the stile ahead and turn right uphill with the fence on your left. Cross the stile at the top of the field and continue uphill on the clear path. Cross the stile in the fence at the top, go through the gate in the wall ahead and walk straight up the grassy path. This bears slightly right round holly trees. Ignore a large wooden gate in the hedge on the left and follow the hedge round to a stile.

Walk forward up the High Austby access drive and at the T-junction turn right. Where this narrow tarmac road turns right go straight ahead along the track. At Tivoli the road once more becomes tarmac. On reaching rhododendron woodland a detour can be made through a gate on the left (signposted Calvary) to view some mid 19th-century Italian Stations of the Cross, then return to the track. The track emerges from the wood and turns right. Follow it down past the houses. The large house half right is Middleton Lodge, dating from c.1600, now a monastery. The track turns left again and reaches a road.

Turn left and in a few yards right along the road to Middleton. In 130 yards cross a stile on the right and bear very slightly left downhill to a signpost and stile into Middleton Woods. These woods are owned by Bradford Council and you may walk where you like in them. There are many paths, and route-finding can be a problem. Walk down into the woods, after 25 yards keeping left at a fork. Immediately after crossing a small beck, keep left at another fork, soon crossing another slightly larger beck. Now you walk roughly parallel to the boundary fence of the wood up on the left, keeping always on the main path, all the way to the exit from the wood, which you leave over a stile a short distance to the left of a house painted white.

Cross the road to the stile opposite and take the middle of the three paths which present themselves, the one which bears left and descends. When you reach a variety of cross paths, bear right for a short distance then take a clear path forking left. Shortly you cross over a cross path and drop quite steeply. At the foot of the slope cross a beck and bear left. Keep always on the main path which descends gently to reach the next road opposite the suspension bridge. Cross the bridge and turn right along the riverside path which you follow back to the main road bridge in Ilkley. Climb the steps and turn left for the town centre.

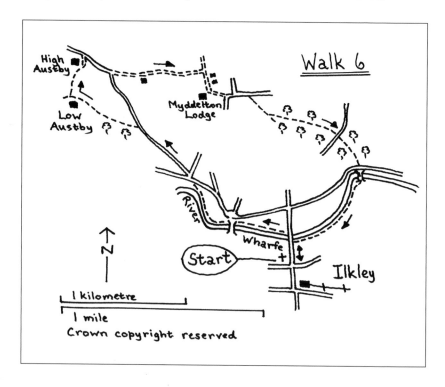

BURLEY IN WHARFEDALE TO BURLEY MOOR

WALK 7

4.3 miles (7 km); Explorer 27. Field and moorland paths and old tracks; superb views of Lower Wharfedale.

The walk starts at Burley in Wharfedale station. There are trains from Bradford, Leeds and Ilkley, and there is parking at the station. If you arrive from Bradford or Leeds, leave the station by the exit halfway along the platform. If coming from Ilkley, or starting from the car park, cross the railway by the footbridge and leave the station by the exit halfway along the platform.

On leaving the station, turn left along the tarmac lane. This is Hag Farm Road, and you must follow it all the way to its end at Hag Farm. It loses its tarmac surface on the way. Where the track makes its final curve right to the farm, fork left along another track with a fence on the right to a stile by a gate. Follow the track down with a wall on the left. On reaching a gap-stile in this wall, turn sharp right and walk uphill with the beck on your left. The path leads to a gap-stile into a field. Continue by the wall/fence on your left to another stile, then keep following the fence to a stile in it. Cross the footbridge and follow the path to some steps, at the top of which bear right up the steep access drive.

Cross over the road through Burley Woodhead into the track opposite, but after 60 yards at a marker post ford the beck on the left and follow the clear path uphill, soon in an old hedged way. Go through a gate at the end and turn right with a wall on the right, but where this begins to bend right, keep forward up a clear grassy path. This soon peters out, but keep on up the grass to reach a cross track at a footpath sign. Turn right along it. Having picked up a wall on the right, follow it to a stile by a gate, and 20 yards beyond keep right at the fork. Keep right also at the next fork (there is a small brick building between the branches) and soon the track bends right and drops to pass a farm with the embankment of Carr Bottom Reservoir up on the left.

At the next farm, York View, from where, it is said, one can see York Minster 25 miles away, do not follow the track through the gate ahead, but turn left and follow another track with a wall on the right. Just before you reach two large barns on the right at the next farm (Crag Top) find a path bearing left across the moor. In a few yards it passes above and to the left of an old quarry. Soon you are walking on a clear path through bracken. The views are magnificent, from Guiseley round to Beamsley Beacon.

Eventually the clear path leads down to cross Coldstone Beck in its ravine. Climb up the other side, but before you reach the top bear right on a descending grassy path. When you reach a cross path turn right and descend with the beck in its deep ravine on your right to join the road on a bend. Bear right down the road, but at the end of the layby on the right take the path over the gorse-covered hillock. It leads back to the road: cross over and walk left for a few yards to take the access road to the Ilkley Moor Garden Centre on the right.

After a few yards ignore the fork right into the garden centre and keep on down the walled access road. At The Lodge keep left with the track, round to the left of the buildings, and follow it as far as its first sharp **left hand** bend. Here fork **right** to pass through a kissing-gate by a large metal gate, and when after a few yards the wall on the left turns sharp left, bear slightly left and walk parallel to the edge of the wood on the left to the next kissing-gate by another large metal gate. Now follow the fence on the right, which soon becomes a wall. Where the wall ends, go through another small wooden kissing-gate and keep forward along the clear path. A stile leads onto a farm access road: keep forward along it. About 80 yards after passing the farm fork left down a fenced path. Join a broad track and bear right along it. At the motor road turn left to return to your starting point.

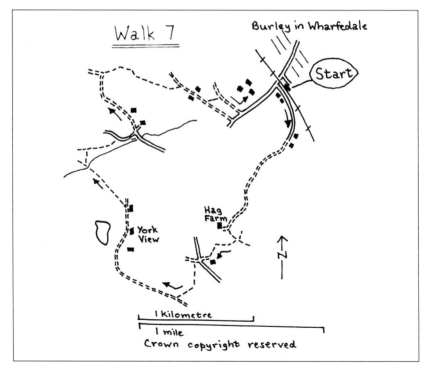

OVER ROMBALD'S MOOR TO DICK HUDSON'S

WALK 8

10 miles (16 km); Explorer 27. A classic moorland ramble from Ilkley. There are so many paths on Ilkley Moor that it is difficult to describe a route clearly, but I have done my best. Please pay close attention to route finding, particularly on the early part of the walk.

The walk starts at the railway/bus station in Ilkley. Trains and/or buses are available from Bradford, Leeds, Keighley and Skipton. If coming by car, from the traffic lights in the centre of Ilkley drive up Brook Street (signposted Ilkley Moor) and at the top bear left then immediately right up the one-way Wells Road; over the cattle grid at the top there is a car park immediately on the right. Park here. Walk back over the cattle grid and turn right along Crossbeck Road for a yard or two, then fork right up a track to a gate onto the moor and join the route description at [*].

Walk along the front of the old railway station building towards the town centre, cross the main road on your left at the pedestrian crossing, turn right for a yard or two then left up Wells Road. At the top cross Crossbeck Road and take the track a few yards to the left of the cattle grid leading forward to a gate onto the moor. [*] Go through the **large** gate (**not** the kissing-gate) and follow the tarmac drive up to The Tarn. Walk round The Tarn in either direction to the far end, where a clear path leads through a small rock outcrop. Follow this to the footbridge over Backstone Beck, cross and take the broad stepped path up the other side.

Soon you are walking parallel to the road down below on the left. Ignore paths forking left downhill, and you will reach a broad cross track. Turn right up this into the trees. Shortly after entering the trees you reach another cross track: turn left uphill. When the gradient eases, with the Cow and Calf rocks ahead, bear right along the rim of the quarry and follow it until you reach a broad cross track. Turn right along this, soon bearing left away from the quarry on a good path. In a few yards another good path comes in from the left. Keep forward on the gently ascending path. Take the next very clear path forking left, and after a few yards again keep left at a fork. In a few yards further turn left along a clear cross path, and a few yards further on turn right up a clear **grassy** path. In a few yards cross over another cross path and keep on uphill, parallel to the ravine over to your right.

The broad grassy path soon bears slightly left away from the ravine and reaches a very clear cross track. Turn left along this, heading for a single large boulder. The track passes to the right of this. Shortly afterwards, where the track makes a sharp left hand bend, fork right off it on a clear broad path. At the next fork keep right, heading up the slope towards a cluster of boulders. Here there is a yellow post marking the boundary

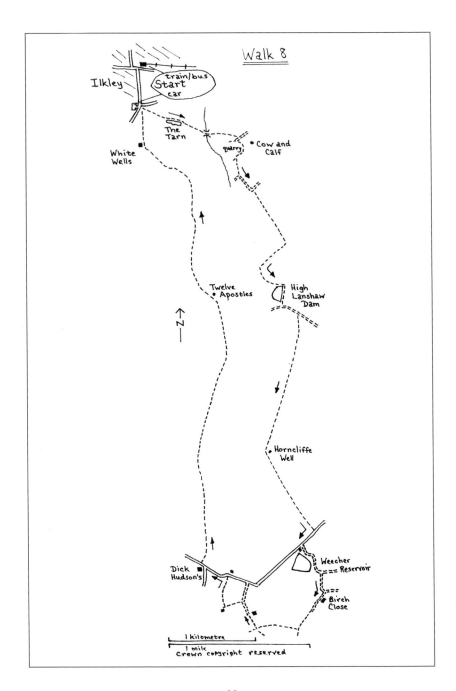

Walk 8

Ilkley

train/bus
Start
car

The Tarn

quarry

• Cow and Calf

White Wells

• Twelve Apostles

High Lanshaw Dam

N ↑

• Horncliffe Well

Dick Hudson's

Weecher Reservoir

Birch Close

1 kilometre

1 mile
Crown copyright reserved

between Ilkley and Burley parishes. Follow the clear path over the moor towards the next two boundary markers, after which it bends left towards a small reservoir. Having passed to the left of the reservoir turn right over the embankment (High Lanshaw Dam). At the far end cross a wet patch by walking along the top of a stone culvert, then climb the slope and at the top turn left along a clear path, soon being joined by another clear path from the right. Immediately after the next outcrop of rocks on the right and 80 yards before an old railway wagon, turn right on a narrow path which passes the left hand end of the rocks and bears slightly left over the moor. **It is essential to find this path**, which is narrow but quite clear. After a time you are walking parallel to a fence over on the left, beyond which there are extensive views.

There are two or three little becks to be crossed on the way, but there are always stepping stones, and there are some wet patches, but the route is never in doubt and the fence is an infallible guide. Eventually the path leads to a stile in a cross wall. Cross it. Another stile immediately to the left gives access to the Horncliffe Well, where there are several inscribed stones, but our route turns left down a clear cross path, which is followed to the next motor road, crossing one stile on the way.

Turn right along the road, which is narrow and busy and there is no footway, for 200 yards, and just before a cottage on the left turn left down a tarmac lane. Pass to the left of Weecher Reservoir, and on reaching a junction with an unsurfaced track, bear right with the tarmac lane uphill. The tarmac ends at a T-junction. Turn right, pass along the back of the houses at Birch Close, go through the gate at the far end and continue along a walled lane. When you are joined from the right by a grit and sand gallop, keep forward along it.

About 90 yards after the wall on the right ends, you pass at present a long metal trough (there is a solitary tree 20 yards to the right). At this point fork half right over the grass, there is no clear path, pass about 10 yards to the left of the tree, aiming just to the right of a mill chimney you can see in the far distance. Soon you will see half right a modern house with a large pale blue barn beside it. Head for a point in the middle between the chimney and this house! As a further help, you will see that power lines cross the field ahead of you, and that you are heading for a point halfway between two of the poles. By this time you should have joined a clear path.

Just before you reach the wall on the far side of the field, cross a gallop to a stile in the wall, ignoring a wooden ladder-stile a few yards to the right. Cross the stile and walk straight over the field to a signpost at a wall corner. Here you join the Bradford-Ilkley Dales Way Link, which you follow all the way back to Ilkley. At the sign turn right and follow the wall on your left through two gates (the modern houses and barn are along to the right at this point) and keep straight on along the access road.

After about 150 yards, where the track bends slightly right, cross the stile in the wall on the left and follow the left hand edge of the field. When you reach the rushes, you pass a short section of wall with an old stile in it. Continue to the next field corner, with trees ahead; ignore the stile ahead and turn right, to follow the wall on your left. Where this turns sharp left, keep straight on up the field, bearing very slightly right, aiming for a house at the top. The stile is slightly to the left of the house. Cross and turn left along the road to Dick Hudson's pub.

A few yards after the pub go through the gated stile on the right, signposted Dales Way Bradford-Ilkley Link, and walk up the walled lane. There are no problems of route finding, and you follow this ancient route all the way back to Ilkley. There are fine views back over Airedale. Notice a few remains of causeying. There is a stile in the boundary wall between Bingley and Burley parishes. On approaching the watershed, just as views over Wharfedale begin to open up, the Bronze Age Twelve Apostles stone circle is on the right of the path.

Soon afterwards you reach a large cairn and the path begins to descend. Over to the left is a boundary stone known as the Lanshaw Lad. Just as Ilkley comes into view below you cross a cross path and continue descending. On reaching White Wells you may like to visit the café and 18th-century bath house. Then take the flight of steps beside the building, from which a clear path descends steeply to the kissing-gate beside the large gate by which you entered the moor at the start of the walk.

White Wells

EAST AND WEST MORTON, SUNNY DALE AND MICKLETHWAITE

WALK 9

7 miles (11 1/4 km); Explorer 27, Pathfinder 682. Old farmhouses and cottages, a leg-stretching track on the southern edge of Rombalds Moor and fine views of Airedale. The Bingley Five Rise Locks on the 127-mile Leeds and Liverpool Canal, which was started in 1770 and opened to through traffic in 1816, the locks being built in 1774, are one of the wonders of the British canal system. Perhaps you will be lucky enough to see a narrow boat locking through.

The walk starts at Canal Road, Crossflatts. If coming by bus, 662/663/665 Bradford-Keighley (frequent), 727/728/729 Keighley-Bingley-Cullingworth (hourly), 760 Keighley-Leeds (half-hourly) will drop you at Canal Road, By train, from Crossflatts Station turn right along the main road and right again up Canal Road. By car, drive up Canal Road and park near the top.

The Canal at Five Rise Locks

From the top of Canal Road walk up to the Leeds and Liverpool Canal and turn left along the towpath. At the second bridge (198A) cross the canal, and in 10 yards go through the stile on the right and follow the fenced path, which ends at the top of a long flight of steps with a stile into a field. Continue across the field, with the valley of Morton Beck to the right, and Micklethwaite beyond. Follow the wall on the left to East Morton. Cross the stile by the gate and walk forward along the road for 50 yards, then take the first street on the left.

Cross the main road at the top and turn left (the Busfeild Arms is to the right) past the public toilets and opposite the post office fork right through the gardens (Albert's Square), climb the few steps and take the second of the two streets on the right. After the tarmac ends, follow the unsurfaced track to the top of the hill. Cross over a cross track, and

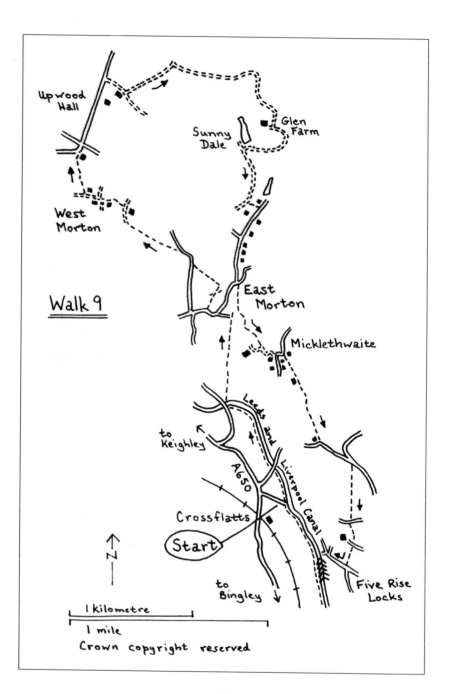

Upwood Hall

Sunny Dale

Glen Farm

West Morton

Walk 9

East Morton

Micklethwaite

to Keighley

Leeds and Liverpool Canal

A650

Crossflatts

Start

to Bingley

Five Rise Locks

N

1 kilometre

1 mile

Crown copyright reserved

passing to the right of the entrance to a bungalow (Stone Haven) follow the path past a terrace of houses then turn left into an enclosed path. At the next road turn right for 150 yards and, ignoring the double metal gate on the left, go through the next gate on the left and walk along the track with the wall on your left.

Go through the gateway ahead and bear right along the wall on your right. Go through another gateway and keep on by the wall. Through another gateway, follow the track ahead: the wall on the right turns right, but soon there is a broken wall on the left. The view half left is to Keighley. Go through the stile by the gate ahead into a walled lane. When this turns right through a gate, cross the stile by the gate ahead and follow the wall on the left to the next stile and another walled lane. Bear

Little Lane, East Morton

right along it, but where it ends turn right and follow the wall on the right to Dene Hole Farm. Go through the gate and walk straight through the yard, which you leave by a stile beside another gate.

Walk up the access road for 15 yards, and just after the entrance to Dene Cottage take the path on the left through the trees and follow the short walled lane to a stile into a field. Follow the wall on the left to West Morton and there walk forward over the grass to the tarmac lane. When the tarmac ends at a junction, keep forward along the track opposite. Immediately after the last house, but before the outbuildings, go through the gap-stile on the right, walk along the side of the house to the next stile, cross the beck, then another stile, and walk up the field with the wall on your right. At the top turn left with the wall, ignore a gateway on the right and cross the stile in the next corner, then turn right up the edge of the next field, near the top bearing left to the prominent step-stile in front of the farm. Walk up the enclosed path, then the farm access road, keep forward up the next motor road and go straight over Street Lane at the crossroads.

Pass Upwood Hall and at the end of the wood take the farm access track on the right. At the farm pass to the left of a very long barn, at the end of which a track comes out of the farmyard on the right and there is a stile by the gate ahead: ignore both of these and turn left on another track with a wall on the right. Follow this clear track, which is quite near the southern edge of Rombalds Moor, all the way to the next farm. On the way you cross Bradup Beck (look left to see the old bridge). At Glen Farm the track passes through a gateway to the left of the buildings and turns left. Follow it down into Sunny Dale, passing a former mill reservoir and the remains of the mill in the woods on the way.

A picturesque corner in East Morton

The track leads across the embankment of Sunny Dale Reservoir. At the junction turn left, and keep on the track until you reach a prominent wall corner on the left. Here turn left and follow the wall down to a stile in the next corner. Keep on down to the next stile, and a few yards further on turn right along a tarmac lane. Follow this all the way to the junction with the main road in East Morton. Cross and turn left for a few yards, then take the cobbled lane on the right (Little Lane). Walk straight through a yard and pass the side of a house into a walled footpath. Walk past the side of another house and at the T-junction turn left (Cliffe Mill Fold) for 20 yards, then turn right down another enclosed path.

Cross Morton Beck by the footbridge and continue up the walled path. The access road from Holroyd Mill joins you from the right and soon the lane turns left past houses. At the end turn right and walk up to the motor road through Micklethwaite. Turn left uphill, at the fork keeping right with the tarmac road, but where this bends sharp left, go through the small gate on the right of the entrance into The Bungalow and turn left to walk across two fields to Fairlady Farm. Pass to the left of the farmhouse, through two stiles by gates and on with a wall on the right to pass through a small gate and into a walled path. There are pleasant views over the Aire valley.

On reaching the next road, cross with care and turn left uphill. At the top keep forward along Lady Lane, but in a few yards go through a small gate on the right and walk down through the woods (owned by the Woodland Trust). After a time the path is between walls. At the next road cross straight over into Pinedale, at the end of which the enclosed path continues. On crossing the next lane, look right for a glimpse of Gawthorpe Hall, built c.1595, the seat in the Middle Ages of the Lords of the Manor. Follow the path down to another access road, walk down this and turn right along the next road.

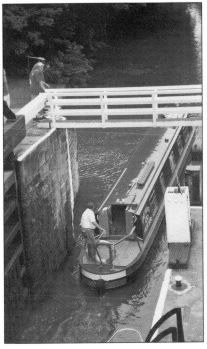

"Off we go…"

At the next junction turn left down Beck Lane, which leads back to the canal at the Five-Rise Locks. On the right here is the Five-Rise Locks Café. Cross the canal and turn right along the towpath. From here it is a short walk back to Canal Road and the start of the walk.

AROUND BAILDON MOOR

WALK 10

6½ miles (10½ km); Pathfinder 682 & Explorer 27. Bluebell woods, a delightful valley, old tracks and farmhouses and fine views. Baildon Moor is a large area of open access land, much of the boundary of which is shown on the Explorer map, Baildon Bank an impressive escarpment.

The walk starts at the Memorial Fountain in the centre of Baildon. There is a Pay & Display car park nearby and Baildon is served by buses 657/658/659/660/661 Bradford-Baildon (frequent).

Walk up Hallcliffe, passing the Parish Church, and at the pair of mini-roundabouts keep straight forward over Heygate Lane into Ladderbanks Lane. The footway ends and the road narrows. When you reach the end of a street on the right, bear left down the narrow footpath. Follow it down between old hedges to reach a gate into a field. Bear slightly right down the slope to the reservoir and turn left along its bank. There is a cricket ground on the left. Cross the leat supplying the reservoir, then the beck by the footbridge, and turn left. This delightful path is rarely beside the beck, but always within earshot of it. On your way through the woods, a mass of bluebells in spring, you cross several side becks and one stile.

After crossing a second stile you are close to the beck, and in a few yards you must cross it by stepping stones. In a few yards the path forks: ignore the stile ahead and fork right (signposted Sconce Lane). The path keeps parallel to the beck on the right for some distance, but at a caravan site on the opposite bank it climbs away from it to reach a stile in the wall on the left. It is in fact a double stile, forward then right, then you turn left up the field edge with a wall to your left to another stile in the top corner. Bear left along the edge of the field, soon turning right with the wall. (A diversion has been applied for on the following section of path as far as the tarmac drive: look out for waymarks.) Follow this wall, then fence, then wall again to cross a stile in the wall ahead into the garden of a house. Walk forward to pass to the right of the house and through a gate in the fence ahead. Continue through the next garden to the facing fence, where you turn left through the white gate and along a ginnel to a tarmac drive.

Bear right up to the motor road and turn right along it. Where the road bends right, fork left off it up Sconce Lane, and follow this until it bends right and then left to pass through Faweather Grange. At the junction of tracks turn left along a track which passes to the right of a row of houses. On the way to the next farm look back and left for extensive views to Leeds and beyond. As you approach Birch Close Farm, ignore a tarmac road coming in from the right and keep forward to pass to the right of the buildings and through the gate at the far end into a walled track, soon joining a gallop. Walk along the edge to avoid the deep grit and sand surface.

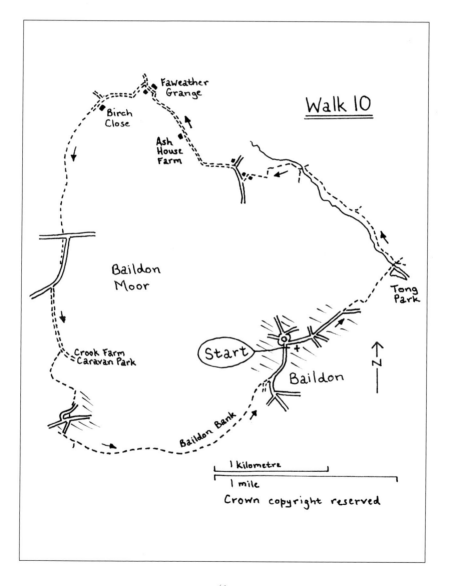

The gallop curves left and comes to a crossing: keep straight on, but where the gallop curves right and another one comes in from the left, cross the stile by the gate ahead and walk forward along the track, veering slightly right to pick up a broken wall. Keeping this wall on your right, follow it to the next road. This section of moorland can be very wet. Pass through a small gate just to the right of a cattle-grid, cross the road to another gate opposite, and keep forward along the path which is parallel to Glen Road on the left. The path joins the road at a wall corner. Walk along the road for about 100 yards and take the access road to Crook Farm Caravan Park on the left. The view right is to Eldwick. A few yards before the entrance to the caravan park turn right off the track on a descending path which soon bends left and reaches a stile by a gate in a wall.

Walk straight across the next field parallel to the fence and caravan park on the left to pass through a gateway, then continue your line to pass through a kissing-gate, then on with the fence/wall on your left to the next field corner. Here ignore the stile on the left and turn right down the wallside. About halfway down take the gate/stile on the left, then continue down the footway. When the road bends right, fork left off it to a stile and walk down the ginnel, crossing another stile on the way.

Cross the next road and go down Rylstone Road opposite. At the bottom turn left along the walled footpath. At a fork keep left. Cross over the bottom of a street and continue along the walled path. Walker Wood and then Midgeley Wood are to one's right. After passing through a metal barrier, where a track comes in from the left, keep straight on with a wall on your right. The path now descends gently. Follow it down until you are about 150 yards from the houses, then take a clear path forking left and climbing again. The view right is to Saltaire and Shipley. On reaching the top of the slope, keep forward on a narrow contouring path along Baildon Bank.

The path sometimes climbs a little, sometimes passes close to the foot of the crags. A steep flight of steps with a handrail comes down from the left. Keep forward on the clear path along the foot of the crags, 30 yards after the steps come in ignoring a right fork and keeping forward parallel to the crags. The tower of Baildon Parish Church now appears ahead. By the end of an iron railing coming down from the left take the right fork. Drop to reach a tarmac path on a bend: keep right, downhill, and at the foot turn left along the broad tarmac cross path. A little further on fork right down the broad track past houses, and at the road turn left to reach the main road by the Bay Horse. Turn left up the hill to return to the start.

DRUID'S ALTAR, ST.IVES, HARDEN AND MARLEY

WALK 11

7¼ miles (11¾ km); Pathfinder 682, Explorer 27. A gentle climb to a fine viewpoint is followed by clear paths through a well cared for estate, heather moorland and a return to the start on the Airedale Way. Although Bingley was granted its market charter by King John in 1212, like several other of the Airedale towns it was only in the second half of the last century that it grew from a village into an industrial town. A few 17th and 18th century houses survive, such as the White Hart Inn by the mediaeval Parish Church.

The walk starts at Bingley Arts Centre in the centre of Bingley. Bingley can be reached by train from Bradford, Leeds, Keighley and Skipton, and there are several town centre car parks.

From the Arts Centre walk past the stocks, butter cross and market hall, pausing to read the information plaque about them, towards the Ferrands Arms. Turn left in front of the pub amd go through the archway and down the steps to the Riverside Walk. Turn right along it. Opposite a car park on the left a stile on the right gives access to the Ailsa Well. *The well is known to have existed in the 15th century. It was once thought to be a holy well, although there is no record of it being dedicated to any particular saint, and the water was thought to have healing properties; in later years it was valued for the cooking of vegetables. The origin of the name is a mystery, but it may come from Alice Hird, who once lived nearby.* Follow the enclosed path to the B6429 and turn left to cross the Aire by Ireland Bridge. *The present bridge was built in 1686 and widened in 1775; the origin of the name is a mystery.*

Bingley, Market Hall and Butter Cross

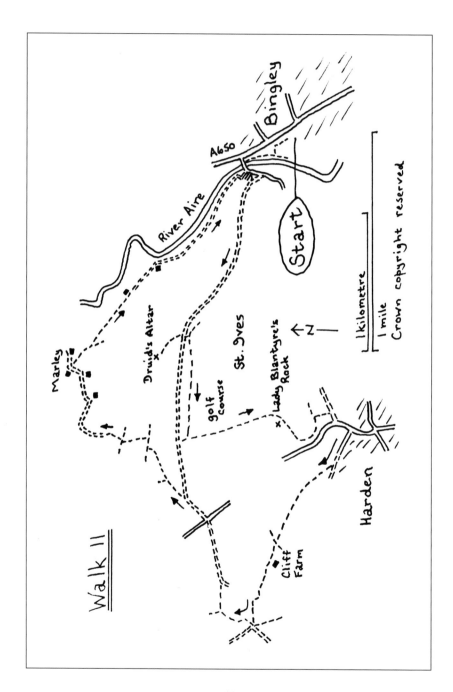

Walk 11

Bingley

A650

River Aire

Start

1 kilometre
1 mile
Crown copyright reserved

N

Marley

Druid's Altar

golf course

St. Ives

Lady Blantyre's Rock

Harden

Cliff Farm

At the Brown Cow cross the road with care and turn right into Ireland Terrace, but immediately fork left up a flight of steps which leads to Altar Lane. Turn right up this track. At the top of the hill you reach a junction of tracks. The walk continues through the gateway on the left with a step-stile beside it, but first fork right, passing to the right of a large wooden gate, signposted "Druid's Altar", on a broad path through the bracken and heather. This soon leads along the edge of the escarpment, with fine views over Airedale. The Druid's Altar is a large outcrop of rock. Retrace your steps and enter the St.Ives Estate, owned by Bradford Council, through the gateway in the wall.

In a few yards turn right through a gap-stile beside an iron gate. The path leads along the left hand edge of the wood to a kissing-gate, then on through the wood. When faced by a wall (there is a tall ladder-stile on the right) turn left. Shortly you reach the Bingley St.Ives golf course and enter a fenced path. After a time the path has a high wall on the left, silver birches on the right and heather moorland beyond. On entering woodland, keep always on the main path. The path begins to descend and steps on the right lead to Lady Blantyre's Rock; a plaque gives information. *The obelisk beyond is in memory of William Ferrand, Lady Blantyre's son-in-law.* Beside it is a picnic table, and this is a pleasant spot for a break.

Return to the main path and continue down it. The path bends left and you are walking parallel to a wall on the right with a road beyond. A few yards after crossing a beck (the bridge has a short stone wall on the right) fork right down a signposted public footpath. On reaching a tarmac drive turn right along it, pass St.Ives Lodge and leave the estate through the gateway. Cross the road and turn left to Harden. In about 150 yards turn right up Moor Edge High Side. When the tarmac ends keep forward along the track. About 100 yards before the next houses go up some steps on the right to a stile and bear half left up the field to the next stile in the wall in front of a wood. A clear path leads up through the wood, soon with a wall on the right. There are fine views back and to the right. When the wall turns sharp right, keep forward on a clear path through the heather. In a few yards keep right at a fork and a short distance further on at another fork keep left, and on reaching a clear cross path turn left along it.

The path is parallel to a clough on the left. About 200 yards before the end of the heather and bracken keep left at a fork. Go through a stile and keep forward through the trees, soon turning left on a path with a wall on the right, but after a few yards cross a stile on the right between two large gateposts. Bear half left up the field, aiming to the right of the large farmhouse (Cliff Farm). Go through the large gate ahead, just to the left of a narrow strip of wood and bear slightly left up the next field to a stile in the top corner. Follow a high wall on the right, but when this turns right keep forward over the field to the next stile. Turn right along a grassy track which in a few yards passes through a gate, then bear half left over the next field to a step-stile in the next wall. Now turn right along the wall on your right to the next stile in the field corner, then again bear half left over the next field to the next stile and keep your line across the next field towards a large metal gate out onto a track.

About 15 yards before this gate cross a stile in the wall on the right and turn right along the wall on your right. At the next corner turn left with the wall, ignoring a gate and stile ahead. Pass to the right of an old quarry and follow the wall into a walled lane. Cross a stile and continue along the lane, which soon bends right (ignore a stile on the left here) and joins a track from Heatherglen Farm. Keep forward to the motor road and cross straight over into another walled track, but when it curves right and passes through a wall (this is Altar Lane again and would be a short cut back to Bingley) keep straight ahead through a kissing-gate and walk down the left hand edge of the field. When the wall bends left keep your line forward across the field (there is no path) and drop to join a track just in front of a cross wall.

Turn right along this track, but when the wall turns left go with it and descend to the bottom of the next field. Go through a gap in the facing wall and immediately turn right over a stile. You have now joined the Airedale Way, which you will follow back to Bingley. Bear half left on a path down through bracken and heather, soon bearing left on a clearer path which comes down from the right. The path leads down to a stile by a metal gate. Follow the track downhill (ignoring a track on the right which leads to a gate), passing two houses, to reach the houses at Marley at the foot of the hill. Turn right, but in a yard or two fork right over a small bridge, cross a stile and follow a grassy track with a beck to your left. *Marley is a historic settlement; the Hall on your left was built in 1627.*

Go through the kissing-gate beside the large white gate and continue along the track. Where it forks keep left, pass through a gateway and follow the track along the right hand edge of the field with a wood on the right. Pass to the right of the next house, Cophurst, and continue on the track to the next house, Ravenroyd. Pass to the left of it and bear left down the access road. Where it forks, keep left on the lower track close to the Aire. A few yards before you reach Ireland Bridge you must turn right along a cobbled street, then in a few yards left along Ireland Street, which leads back to the B6429. Turn left over the bridge to return to the centre of Bingley.

HARDEN MOOR AND THE WORTH WAY

WALK 12

5 miles (8 km); Pathfinder 682. A walk with superb views, a stretch of heather moorland, old tracks and paths, many remains of the quarrying which was such an important industry last century, and a section of the Worth Way.

The walk starts in picturesque Hainworth (GR 059 391). Either park courteously in the centre of the hamlet or use the infrequent M5 bus from Keighley (3 buses a day).

Walk through the hamlet, passing to the right of the old school and admiring the old cottages. When the tarmac ends keep on along the track. Having left the main part of the hamlet, just before you reach some more houses, the track forks. Keep left uphill, following the waymark which tells you that you are on the Worth Way. There are fine views right over the Worth

Hainworth

valley. Soon there is lots of evidence of quarrying on the left. Follow this track all the way to the next motor road and keep forward along this into Barcroft. Shortly after passing a garage on the left fork left up a tarmac lane, here leaving the Worth Way.

The lane bends left and you are joined by the Senior Way. When the houses end, the tarmac ends too, and you keep on along the track. It descends gently for some distance. Take the first left fork, a double track with grass in the middle, past a sign which says No Cycling: Footpath Only. On reaching the farm keep straight forward, pass to the left of the farmhouse and continue along a grassy ride with a wood over the wall on the left and young trees on the right. At the end of the wood go through a stile into a field and follow the wall on your left along.

Follow this wall all the way to the Cullingworth-Keighley road; the last section is in an old walled lane. Cross the road and turn left for just over

100 yards to a signposted bridleway on the right which passes round a wooden barrier and along a walled lane. The view right is to Cullingworth. Pass through a stile by a gate and ignore a path forking left through a kissing-gate onto the moor. Pass Hunter Hill Farm on the right, pass round a large wooden gate and follow the wall on your left to the Ryecroft Road. There is a fine view right over the valley of Harden Beck.

Cross the road and take the track opposite through the houses of Ryecroft, ignoring in a short distance a signposted path on the right. Keep on the track all the way through the houses, passing Ryecroft Farm, and through old iron gates and on along a track. The view right is to Harden and Bingley beyond. Pass through a large and a small gate at a house called Woodhead, then fork left off the track on a clear narrow ascending path parallel to the wall on the left. A stile leads out onto Harden Moor.

Harden Moor is an Access Area, where you may walk where you wish. It is also a place where it is easy to get lost - one pile of quarry waste is much like another and the area is criss-crossed by paths - so I have chosen a route which is above all easy to follow. So keep forward on a clear path through the bilberries and heather. On reaching a clear fork turn right on a path which crosses a shallow valley and heads towards two pylons on the skyline. But after just over 100 yards turn very sharply left along another clear path. It ascends. Keep always on the main path. You reach a crossing of paths, where the one on the left goes very soon very steeply down into a little gulley: ignore this and keep straight on.

Ignore the next path forking off right, but a yard or two after that keep right at another fork and head towards old quarry spoil heaps. A few yards before you reach them you come to a junction of paths. Take care here. The path straight ahead goes up into the spoil heaps: ignore it, and turn slightly right and take the next path on the right, which passes to the right of the first spoil heap and then between two more ahead. Before you get to these two, you will find the remains of paving stones on the path, showing that this was a path used by quarrymen long ago. Keep following this intermittently paved path. Another path joins you from the left. Keep forward. Now your problems are over, for you are going to follow this very clear path all the way to the far edge of the moor.

Further along you can detect hollows in the paving stones, where cart wheels have worn the stone away. On the way you cross straight over a very clear cross path. Leave the moor through a gap by a gate and walk forward to join the stony track. Keep straight on along it. Very extensive views open up ahead, to Haworth, Keighley and beyond. Follow the track, then lane, down to the next motor road, cross it and turn right down the footway. On the next bend, with Keighley spread out before you, turn left down a track, tarmac at first. Take the next track forking left. On reaching the house, keep following the wall on the left to a step-stile, then continue by the wall on the left. Cross the stile in the field corner and turn right into the next field, follow the wall on the left down, and turn left through the first gateway in it, to walk along the right hand edge of the next field. This is where you rejoin the Worth Way.

Pass through the next stile, then walk straight over the next field to the next stile opposite, then continue with a wall on the right. Go through the next stile and keep on by the wall on your right, but in the far corner of the field go through the stile on the right beside the gateway and in a yard or two turn left to follow the wall on the left to Hainworth.

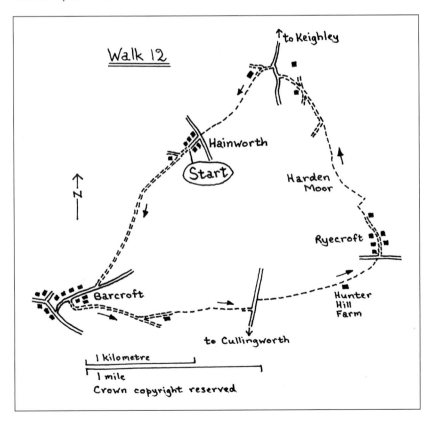

Walk 12

to Keighley

Hainworth

Start

Harden Moor

Ryecroft

Barcroft

Hunter Hill Farm

to Cullingworth

1 kilometre

1 mile

Crown copyright reserved

N

THREE MORE WALKS IN THE HAWORTH AREA

The Worth Way

The Worth Way is an 11-mile circular walk from Keighley Station, via Hainworth, Barcroft, Oxenhope (the halfway point) and Haworth. It passes close to all the stations on the Keighley and Worth Valley Railway line, and it uses a variety of public footpaths, from the Victorian ginnels of industrial Keighley to windswept moorland, contouring tracks with superb views, the intimate beauties of the valley of Bridgehouse Beck and the lush pastures of Oakworth.

The Railway Children Walk

A 5-mile circular walk from Haworth Station, devised to enable walkers to visit the various locations used in the film "The Railway Children", including the Children's Station (Oakworth), Perks's House, "Three Chimneys", the children's Yorkshire home, with the gap-stile which Perks has difficulty negotiating, the Doctor's House, the Ironmonger's Shop and the Tunnel where Jim injured his leg running in the paper chase.

The Senior Way

A 9½-mile circular walk around Cullingworth, starting and finishing at Hallas Bridge. On the way the walk passes Goit Stock waterfalls, Brow Moor, Hallas Rough Park and Hewenden Reservoir and Viaduct.

Leaflets about all these walks are obtainable from local TICs.

THE BRONTË WAY

The Brontë Way is a long-distance footpath of some 43 miles (kilometres) from Oakwell Hall, Birstall, near Leeds in West Yorkshire to Gawthorpe Hall, Padiham in Lancashire. It links together a variety of places which played a part in the lives and literary productions of the Brontë family, embracing paths which must have been used by the Reverend Patrick Brontë as he went about his ministry and others used by his daughters when they were visiting friends or taking walks in the countryside which inspired their novels. It also offers an attractive introduction to the pastoral and moorland landscapes of the South Pennines.

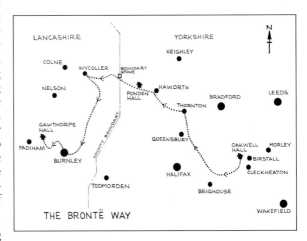

THE BRONTË WAY

The West Riding Area of the Ramblers' Association has published a guide to the Brontë Way, written by Marje Wilson. It covers the whole route in a series of eleven circular walks, for each of which there is a detailed description and a sketch map, and there are clear directions for reaching the starting points, both for those using public transport and for motorists.

Marje Wilson, *The Brontë Way* costs £4.50 and is widely available from local bookshops and TICs.

Oakwell Hall, the Elizabethan Manor House which featured as "Fieldhead" in Charlotte Brontë's *Shirley*, and the nearby Red House Museum, once the home of Charlotte's friends, the Taylors, and which she featured as "Briarmains" in *Shirley*, are open all year, Mon-Fri 11.00-17.00, Sat/Sun 12.00-17.00.

Gawthorpe Hall, built in 1600-05 and restored by Sir Charles Barry in the 1850s, was the home of the Shuttleworth family. Charlotte became a good friend of Lady Kay Shuttleworth and visited her in the Hall. Gawthorpe, which is now owned by the National Trust, is open from Easter to the end of October daily except Monday and Friday, 13.00-17.00.

ANES AROUND OXENHOPE

WALK 13

Pathfinder 682 or Outdoor Leisure 21. A high level ope, mainly on old tracks, with superb views. At there is a charming café in an old railway carriage, pubs on the route of the walk.

The ⌐.⌐ ⌐s at Oxenhope Station on the Keighley & Worth Valley line. ⌐⌐e car park here is for rail users only, so I suggest that drivers take the B6141 Denholme road out of Oxenhope; just after the end of the 30 mph limit there is an unofficial layby on the left. Either park here, or a short distance before that turn left up Black Moor Road then fork left into Height Lane, where there is a layby 200 yards along on the left. In this case walk back to the B6141. In both cases start the walk at [*].

Leave the station and take the first minor road on the left. Follow it up to the main road and cross diagonally left to ascend Dark Lane. When the gradient eases, keep straight forward at the junction. As you get higher, glorious views open up over Oxenhope and much of the route of your walk. After a time Leeming Reservoir comes into view below on the right. Follow this lane all the way to the next motor road and turn right.

On reaching the B6141 bear left along it. [*] About 100 yards before the Dog & Gun cross the signposted stile on the right and bear half left over the field to a gap-stile in the next wall, then again half left up the next field to a stile onto a tarmac lane. Turn right up this through the hamlet of Sawood. The lane bends left and climbs to Cobling Farm, where the tarmac surface ends. Keep on along the track and pass through a metal gate. Here you briefly join the Brontë Way. Keep forward along the tarmac lane, but where the tarmac bends left into the grounds of Thornton Moor Reservoir, keep forward along the stony track.

On the next left hand bend the Brontë Way forks off right, but stay on the track for another 50 yards to a clear fork, and keep right on the clear descending track. Follow it all the way to the next motor road and turn right along it. Cross the cattle grid and pass the transmitter, after which the road bends right. About 150 yards after this cross the signposted stile on the left and follow the wall on the left through two fields to the next stile and a broad walled lane. Turn left up this and follow it to the A6033, which you reach through the car park of the Wagon & Horses.

Cross the main road, pass through the concrete gateposts and walk along the track, which soon bends right and descends steeply. When the track turns right towards a house, cross the step-stile to the left of the gate ahead and walk down by the wall on the left. Ignore the gateway ahead and bear

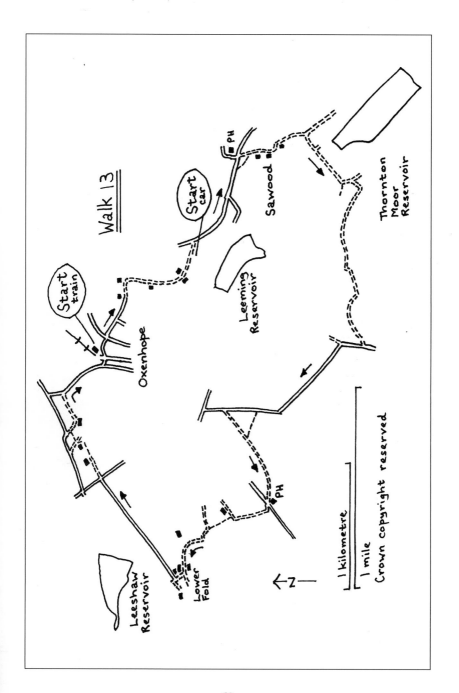

Walk 13

Start car

Start train

Oxenhope

PH

Sawood

Leeming Reservoir

Thornton Moor Reservoir

Leeshaw Reservoir

Lower Fold

PH

← N —

1 kilometre

1 mile

Crown copyright reserved

right with the wall until you reach a stile in it. Over this walk straight down the next field to the next gap-stile, then bear slightly right down the next field to a gap-stile near the foot of the wall on the right. Turn left along the old walled lane. Cross the footbridge at the bottom and continue up the narrow walled lane. Notice the remains of causeying.

Oxenhope Station

At the top of the slope the lane bends left to Lower Fold Farm. At the farm turn right along the track, and at the end of the first building on the right turn sharp right at the fork. The road soon bends right. Leeshaw Reservoir is down to the left. Follow the lane all the way to the next motor road and cross straight over into the track opposite. Pass to the right of the first house, through the small gate ahead, on with the wall on the right to a gated stile into a field, cross straight over the field on an old paved path, through a stile on the right of the next house, along an enclosed path into a cobbled yard, walk to the far end of this and turn left, then right to reach a track.

Cross straight over to the kissing-gate and follow the wall on the right along, crossing several stiles, to reach a walled lane. Turn right along it. Pass to the left of the first group of buildings, go through the small gate beside the large gate ahead and follow the track through the field. Pass through the stile beside the gate at the far end and follow the track to the next road. Turn right along the footway. At the bottom of the hill turn left along Mill Lane to return to the station.

THORNTON MOOR

WALK 14

4¾ miles (7½ km) if you come by bus; 6½ miles (10½ km) for those coming by car; Pathfinder 682 or Outdoor Leisure 21. A walk mainly on old tracks through rough moorland scenery with splendid views.

For those coming by bus the walk starts at the large mill with the clock tower on the southern edge of Denholme, just before the A629 makes several sharp bends; bus 696/697/698/699 Bradford-Thornton-Denholme (half-hourly) or 502 Keighley-Cullingworth-Denholme-Halifax (hourly) will get you there.

As there is no suitable parking place on the route of the walk, I suggest that those coming by car park at Ogden Water, reached by leaving the A629 Denholme-Halifax road at the Whole Hog pub and driving along Ogden Lane. From the far end of the lowest car park go through the kissing-gate and take the track parallel to the reservoir below on the left. After a time the track begins to climb and soon bears right away from the wood. Ahead you will see the mound of the small underground reservoir of Ogden Kirk. The track leads to the left of this and reaches a metal gate. Pass through and keep forward on the broad path. On reaching a wide wall gap go through and fork right. You have now joined the route of the walk proper and should jump to [*] below.

Take the signposted bridleway beside the clock tower of the large mill, called not surprisingly Clock Lane. At the T-junction at the top turn left. Follow this track to its end, pass through the old revolving stile and bear left to follow the wall on the left to the next road, Long Causeway, which you reach by another revolving stile. Turn right for 180 yards then take the track on the left signposted as a public footpath. Where the main track turns left, cross the stile by the gate ahead and follow a lesser track with a wall on the left. At the next corner turn right and continue following the wall, past a small derelict building, to a gated stile in the next corner. A path leads forward across the rough pasture and brings you to a gate onto a tarmac road. Keep forward along this and turn right at the next T-junction.

You have now joined the Brontë Way. The road bends left, and soon the tarmac bends left again into the grounds of Thornton Moor Reservoir: keep forward along the stony track. The views are superb: over Leeming Reservoir to Oxenhope, but much further, to Keighley, Addingham Moor and the fells on the far side of Wharfedale. On the next left hand bend the Brontë Way forks off right, but we continue for a short distance to

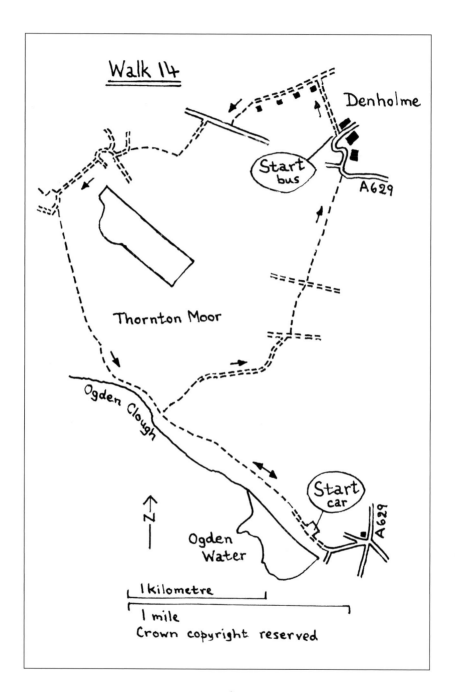

Walk 14

Denholme

Start
bus

A629

Thornton Moor

Ogden Clough

N →

Start
car

A629

Ogden
Water

1 kilometre

1 mile

Crown copyright reserved

another fork. Keep left, passing through the small metal gate beside the large one, onto a climbing track. The wall on the right ends, to be followed by a fence, and when this turns right, keep straight forward on a clear path. The views are splendid. What do you think of the 23 wind turbines?

After a time Ogden Clough develops down on your right and the path follows the edge of it. Further along you will notice a footbridge crossing the beck in the clough and a steep flight of steps on the far side. Ahead of you is a wall with a large gap in it: immediately before this wall turn sharp left. (Motorists will go through the gap and follow their outward route back to Ogden Water.) [*] A grassy track ascends gently over the moor. It leads to a metal gate: go through and continue forward, still on a clear track, which at the top of the next slope bends slightly right. Fine views open up to the left, the right and ahead. You are walking along the old Foreside Lane. Eventually the track descends to a T-junction: turn right through the gateway, but in 20 yards go through the small gate on the left and walk up the field with a wall on your right.

When the wall ends, keep forward, bearing slightly right, to a gated stile onto Thornton Moor Road. Cross to the stile opposite and keep forward with a fence then wall on your right. Pass through the broken wall at the end of the field and keep on, now with the wall on your left. Just before the wall bends left, bear slightly right away from it and continue downhill heading towards the mills in Denholme (no clear path) to reach a gated stile in the wall at the bottom of the field. Walk straight down the next field to a small gate out onto the A629. Cross with care and turn left to return to the start of the walk. Car walkers should now jump to the start of the walk description.

WILSDEN TO HEWENDEN AND WOOD NOOK

WALK 15

4 miles (6¼ km); Pathfinder 682. A delightful stroll, using old tracks and field paths, with fine views.

The walk starts at the Post Office in Wilsden. Bus 690, hourly from Bradford, or 727/728, hourly from Keighley or Bingley, will take you there. If coming by car, park in the Royd House car park on Main Street, making sure you park on the "B" (long-stay) side. If that is full, there is more parking by the Village Hall, reached by driving up Royd Street and turning right along Townfield.

Walk down Main Street for 70 yards and turn left along Cranford Place. When it begins to climb, ignore the gateway ahead and turn right through a wall-gap into a walled footpath. At a crossing of paths, by a concrete lamppost, keep forward along the paved path. When the walled path ends, bear half left up the field, and on reaching the wall on the far side, turn left up it on a paved path to a

Wilsden Hill

stile into a walled track. Keep forward to the tarmac road and turn right through the attractive hamlet of Wilsden Hill.

Walk down the hill and turn left along Tan House Lane. There are pleasant views right to Harden. After a time, by some houses, Tan House Lane becomes Nab Lane and loses its surface. The path climbs, but when the gradient eases the path makes a long left hand curve. The view opens up to Cullingworth, the Hewenden viaduct and Denholme. Just after passing a bench on the left, between the first and second pylons, fork right off the track through a gap-stile and walk down the slope with a wall on your left, passing under the power lines. Go through another stile at the bottom, cross straight over the road and walk down the No Through Road opposite.

When the road bends right, keep straight forward through the gate and down the old mill access road. Bend left with it, but just before it turns sharp right to drop to the mill, go through the stile on the left and walk

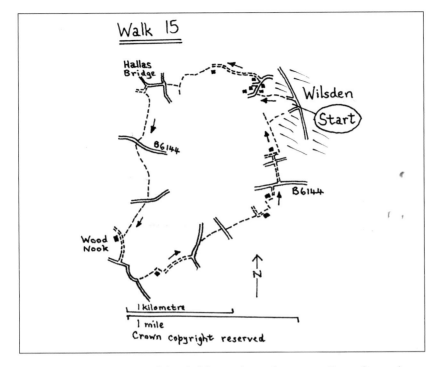

Walk 15

Hallas Bridge

Wilsden

Start

B6144

B6144

Wood Nook

N

1 kilometre

1 mile

Crown copyright reserved

along the bottom edge of the field. Go through a gap-stile and now keep parallel to the fence/wall on the left, passing through another stile on the way. Eventually the clear path bends right downhill to reach a stile in the wall on the left. Walk across the next field to the B6144. Cross diagonally right to the gap-stile opposite (the **nearer** of the two footpath signs).

Now bear left up the slope (no clear path), keeping close to the edge of the steeper ground on the left. Pass through a broken wall and bear left down to the beck and follow it up. Cross a stile in the next cross wall and continue by the beck. Pass through the next cross wall and now bear slightly right away from the beck (you can't at first see where you are heading for) to pass through a large gap in the next wall, then walk straight over the next field to a step-stile out onto a road. Cross diagonally left to the gap-stile opposite. From it bear right to the next stile by an old gateway, and now follow the wall on your right.

Cross straight over a track coming from the farm on the right, through the gap-stile opposite, and keep on by the wall on the right. Cross the stile in the next corner and keep on by the wall. Denholme is straight ahead on the skyline. Follow the wall down to a stile in the bottom

59

corner and turn left along the track. At the next road turn left. The road bends right and soon you can cut a corner by a path on the left. Continue up the road for a few more yards to a footpath sign pointing left to a stile by a gate. Cross it and bear half right quite steeply uphill to the top corner of the field. Cross through the broken wall and keep the same line up through the trees.

Cross the stile in the wall at the top at the left hand end of the farm buildings then follow the wall on your right along to the next stile. Turn left and follow the farm access road to the next motor road. Turn left along it, but a few yards after passing a house on the left cross a stile in the wall on the right and walk along by the wall on the right. Cross straight over the next road to the stile by the gate opposite and follow the wall on your left through two fields. In the third field a stile by

Wilsden Hill

the wall leads into a walled footpath which leads past the house and onto the access road. Follow this along, ignoring a walled track on the left, and walk straight through the next farmyard, looking out for a **small** gate ahead leading into a field. Follow the wall on your right to the next corner, there turning sharp left with the wall.

Pass through a gap in the next wall, cross the stile in the next corner, then follow the wall on the right for a few more yards to a gap-stile in it, go through and follow the wall on your left, with a farm beyond. At the far end of the garden wall on the left go through the small gate on the left, walk through the farmyard and straight down the access road to the B6144. Cross to the footway and turn right. At the end of the cemetery turn left along a track.

At the end of the track cross straight over the cross street and walk along the tarmac lane opposite. When faced by a large house ahead go through the gates **on the right** and walk along the track to reach a narrow enclosed path. This path soon turns sharp left. Look out for where it makes a little kink left, then right again, then when the houses on the right end and there is a large open grassy space ahead, turn sharp right down an old walled lane. When you reach a street, keep forward past the car park of the Bell Inn to return to Wilsden post office.

CHELLOW DEAN

WALK 16

2 miles (3 km); Pathfinder 682. Chellow Dean is a wooded valley which contains two reservoirs constructed in the middle of the last century as Bradford's first water supply. They are no longer used for this purpose, but form part of a Site of Scientific Interest and are managed for recreation and wildlife. This small area forms an oasis of peace, and you cannot do better than follow the signposted and waymarked circular walk (the waymarks are red). This can be done either clockwise or anti-clockwise: my route goes round anti-clockwise. No description is really necessary, but I give the essentials nevertheless.

The Chellow Dean car park is on the B6144 Bradford-Haworth road just before the junction with the B6146 to Cottingley. The 620 Bradford-Cottingley/Bingley bus (half-hourly) passes the car park. There is an information board at the car park.

From the car park take the broad path into the trees, in 150 yards keeping right at the fork. At a signposted cross path keep straight on,

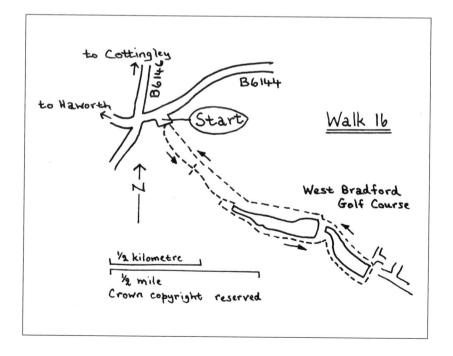

with flights of steps both to left and right, and at the next signposted junction turn right, and soon you have the upper reservoir on your left. Leaving the dam at the far end on your left, keep forward down to the lower reservoir. At the far end of this one turn left over the dam to the keeper's lodge, then left again, still with the reservoir on your left.

At the end of the reservoir fork right up a flight of steps, then bear left up to the level of the upper reservoir. Here turn right up some more steps, but ignore the gap in the wall at the top, instead keeping along the path just inside the wood, with the reservoir down on your left. The path leads through another gap in the wall, and now bear left along the top edge of the wood with West Bradford Golf Course on your right. Soon you are back inside the boundary wall of the wood. Keep straight on, always on the main path, and it will lead you back to the car park.

Remember the Country Code:

Guard against all risk of fire.

Take your litter home. As well as being unsightly, it may be a hazard to livestock.

If you find a gate closed, be careful to close it again behind you. If it is open, leave it open.

Do not pollute streams or rivers, ponds, lakes or reservoirs.

Keep dogs under control: they may frighten other walkers or be a threat to livestock.

Protect, wildlife, plants and trees.

Keep to public paths across farmland.

Take special care on country roads.

Use gates and stiles to cross fences, hedges and walls.

Make no unnecessary noise.

Leave livestock, crops and machinery alone.

Enjoy the countryside and respect its life and work.

NORTHCLIFFE WOODS, 'SIX DAYS ONLY' AND HEATON WOODS

WALK 17

2¾ miles (4½ km); Pathfinder 682. A pleasant rural stroll, largely on woodland paths.

By bus: No. 622/623/624/626 (Huddersfield/Brighouse-Bradford/Bingley, Mon-Sat), 625/627 Brighouse-West Royd/Eldwick, Sun); 655/755 Bradford-Leeds; 649 Bradford-Menston; 650/651/652/653/654/656 Bradford-Otley/Ilkley/Harrogate; 660/661 West Bowling-Bradford-Baildon; 662/663/664/665 Bradford-Keighley/Haworth/Oxenhope/Stanbury. Alight at the Norwood Terrace stop, which is beside attractive gardens forming the grounds of some blocks of flats about 250 yards on the Bradford side of the junction of the A650 (to Bingley) and the A6038 (to Shipley), continue walking away from Bradford and turn left along Cliffe Wood Avenue.

By car: About 250 yards on the Bradford side of the junction of the A650 (to Bingley) and the A6038 (to Shipley) turn into Cliffe Wood Avenue (on the corner is the Cliffwood Guest House) and drive along to the car park.

Walk along to the end of the car park and enter the woods on the wide valley track. Shortly after the tarmac track becomes rough there is a miniature railway on the left, open on summer Sundays. Continue along the beckside for quite a distance. Where the path forks, the right hand branch leading up steps to the large clubhouse of the Northcliffe Golf Club, take the left fork leading across the beck also up some steps. At the top of the slope, keep ahead on the path between two parts of the golf course (still wooded). Keep ahead through a gap-stile into an enclosed path.

At the motor road turn left and follow the road round to a group of 17th-century houses - officially "Heaton Royds" but always known locally as "Six Days Only". Just before the cottages there is a horse trough on the right inscribed "J.Field Esquire". As the road drops steeply take a signposted path on the right leading into the wood high above the beck, Weather Royds Wood. Turn left across the head of the gill, and left again at two old gateposts (ignoring the path descending left into the valley) to follow the track with the beck still down on your left and soon a wall on the right. Reach the next road by a gap-stile beside a gate, cross it diagonally right and enter Heaton Woods through another stile.

After a time you join a broader path and keep straight on along it. On reaching path junctions with two footpath signposts quite close together, keep forward on the main path high above the beck. At another path crossing, when again there are two signposts close together, turn left on a path which soon descends by a few steps. About 20 yards after these turn sharp left on a path which soon descends to the beck by more steps.

Turn right and follow the beck, crossing it by a wooden footbridge at Rocky Crossing. From the bridge bear right for 15 yards, then fork half-left away from the beck on a gently rising path. Keep right at the next T-junction, ignoring the path dropping to the beck. The path keeps parallel to the beck, which is some distance off on the right, and leaves the woods through a barrier. Follow the dirt track to the right of houses. At the tarmac road keep forward, and at the main road turn left to return to the starting point.

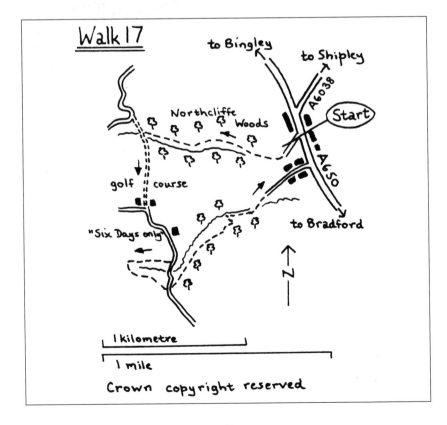

THORNTON TO MOUNTAIN

WALK 18

4 ½ miles (7 km); Pathfinder 682. Old field paths, fine views and a delightful valley. There are also 5 pubs on the route! Thornton is a village with Brontë associations. In 1815 the Revd Patrick Brontë became Perpetual Curate of Thornton and moved with his wife and two young children into the house in Market Street in which, in the space of five years, four more children were born, Charlotte, Branwell, Emily and Anne. Why not visit it before or after your walk?

By bus: 502/503, 697/699, 607 to the junction of Thornton Road and Kipping Lane in Thornton.

By car: From the junction by the Black Horse in the centre of Thornton drive up West Lane and park where it widens.

Walk up Kipping Lane. At the junction, a short detour along Market Street will bring you to the house in which the famous Brontë children were born, but the walk bears left past the Black Horse (the first pub) up West Lane. Cross to the footway on the right hand side going up, and at the top cross the end of Harcourt Avenue and bear right with the footway uphill towards the Sun Inn (the second pub). Just past the pub turn left along Wicken Lane, but in a few yards climb some steps on the right and walk along the right hand edge of the field.

The Brontë Birthplace

On reaching a wall corner at the far end of the cricket ground, go through a wall gap and a stile and now follow the wall on your left. Pass through another two stiles and the path is now paved. Cross another stile, ignore a gateway in the wall on the left and 10 yards further on pass through a stile on the left and follow the wall on your right to the stile in the next corner. Climb some steps, go through the stile at the top, and now the wall is on your left. Cross another stile, pass through a small gate and walk forward to the road. The

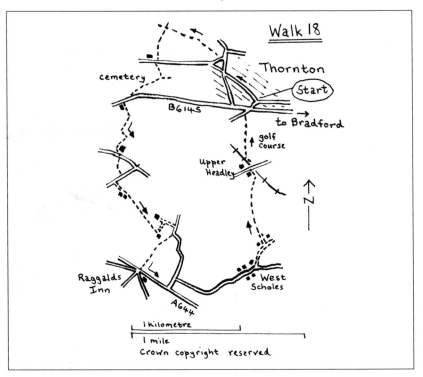

Ring o' Bells (the third pub) is to your right. Cross the road and walk along the left hand edge of the pub car park, soon in an enclosed path.

Pass through a wall gap, cross straight over a track to a gap-stile opposite and walk down the right hand edge of the field. Just after passing through a broken down cross wall, go through a kissing-gate on the right into Thornton Cemetery. After 15 yards fork left on a broad descending tarmac drive and follow it to the entrance to the cemetery on the B6145. Turn right, but opposite the bus turning circle cross the road and walk down through the large car park, leaving it in the bottom right hand corner. Keep straight forward to find a stile into a field. Follow the wall on your right to the next stile, and now go half right, cutting the corner of the next field, to a wall corner. Follow the wall on your left up, in the next corner turn sharp right with it, go through a gap-stile straight ahead and walk along the top edge of the next field.

On reaching a gateway in a facing wall turn left to find a stile on the right in the wall corner. Cross and turn left, with the wall on the left, to the next stile, go right a few yards to the road, then left along Squirrel Lane. Opposite the next house on the left go through a large gate on the right, immediately followed by a small one, and follow the wall on your left along. Where it ends, keep straight forward across the field, aiming well to the right of the pylon, to a stile onto the next road. Turn right, then take the next access road on the left. Follow the track to the left of two houses and go through the large gate ahead. Walk through a small field to the gate at the far end, then walk straight across the next field to the stile in the wall opposite. Continue with the wall on your right.

Go through the gate at the far end of the field, and now bear slightly right away from the wall on the left, towards the left hand end of the buildings of Nettle Hole Farm. Go through the stile to the left of the large gate and walk forward through

Approaching Thornton

the farmyard, then turn left down the access track. Pass through the double gate, turn right and follow the track to the next road (Pit Lane). Turn right, but in a few yards, on the bend, cross the stile in a wall corner on the right and bear half left up the field to the next stile in the wall at the top. Keep straight on up the next two fields, after which you have a wall on the right. Near the top of this field go through a stile on the right beside a gate, turn left to the next stile, and continue with the wall on your right.

Pass through another stile and walk forward to reach the A644 opposite the Raggalds Inn (the fourth pub). Turn left along the road. Shortly after entering Mountain (30 mph) turn left down Pit Lane (again!). Take the next road on the right (Low Lane) and follow it to West Scholes. At the road junction by the Junction Inn (the fifth and final pub) bear left along the front of the pub into a lane, which has preserved some of its old cobbles and setts. The lane descends and bends left. Pass West Scholes Mill, and just after a long low building on the left turn left along a track which passes between houses. Cross a step-stile beside the gate straight ahead.

There now follows perhaps the most delightful part of the ramble. Continue down the walled lane, but a few yards after a large gateway on the left go through a stile on the left and bear right down a shallow gulley to a prominent stile with trees beyond. From the stile a clear track leads downhill to another stile and a footbridge. Over the bridge bear half right up the other side, crossing a stile and climbing towards a tunnel under the old railway line. About 15 yards before the tunnel cross

History underfoot

a stile in the fence on the left, cross diagonally right over the track and climb to another stile on the left near the left hand end of the viaduct. Cross the stile and follow the wall on the right up. The next stile leads into a short stretch of walled path and to Headley Lane.

A short distance up to the left is Upper Headley Farm, one of the oldest houses in the district, but the high wall round it restricts one's view of it. Turn right down the road, but immediately after the bridge climb some steps on the left into a narrow walled lane. Pass through two stiles, with another railway bridge on the left, and follow the walled lane to its end. Pass through the stile and drop steeply (this can be slippery) to Headley Golf Course. Walk straight down across the golf course (beware of flying balls!) - you are close to the famous railway viaduct on the left - pass to the left of the notice board, cross the footbridge and continue up the old paved path. At the road turn right to reach the start of the walk. (Motorists will jump to the start of the walk description for the route back to their car.)

Thornton

HORTON BANK, CLAYTON AND LITTLE MOOR

WALK 19

4 1/2 miles (7 km); Pathfinder 682, 691. Horton Bank Reservoir was started in 1870 as one of the new reservoirs built to provide water for the woollen industry and the expanding population. Horton Bank Country Park, constructed on the site of the former reservoir by Yorkshire Water for the people of Bradford, was opened on 15th July 1997. There are two suggested circular strolls in the Park, a Lakeside Path (30 minutes) and a Scenic Path which takes you to the main features of the Park and includes long flights of steps (60 minutes). The views are magnificent. Many of the original Victorian features have been restored and incorporated into the Park. Fine views are a feature of this walk, which uses old paths to visit Clayton and Clayton Heights.

By bus: 576 Bradford-Halifax (every 10 minutes), 610/612/613 (frequent service) to Horton Bank Top. The bus stop is quite a distance from the access road to Horton Bank Country Park car park. Walk down to the car park.

By car: Park in the Horton Bank Country Park car park off Great Horton Road.

Leave the car park opposite the end of the tarmac access road, pass between two pairs of massive boulders, the lake is down on your left, climb the steps and pass through a gap in the wall. Turn left and walk to the viewing platform, to enjoy the superb views over Bradford and beyond, and to Great Whernside and Buckden Pike in the Dales. From the viewpoint descend the steps, at the foot turn right up a few more steps. In a short distance go down a few more steps, cross a bridge and turn left. At the next fork keep right, with the large building of Thornton View Hospital ahead, and at the next fork keep left for a few yards to leave the Country Park through a stile.

Turn right, pass along the front of the hospital, go through the large metal gates and continue down the access road. Pass through another gateway and follow the road down. Pass the clubhouse of Clayton Golf Club. At the T-junction cross to the footway and turn left. Follow the road as it bends right, then cross it and turn left along Oakleigh Avenue. A few yards beyond Broomcroft turn right along a short ginnel, then keep forward along the street. Cross over the next cross street and follow Victoria Street. Cross over the next street and continue along Gordon Street opposite (unsurfaced), soon bending left to reach another street. Cross diagonally right and enter Clayton Victoria Park, laid out in 1897 to commemorate Queen Victoria's Diamond Jubilee.

Turn right down a few steps, pass round the granite War Memorial, keep the bowling green on your left, and just beyond it turn left to leave the

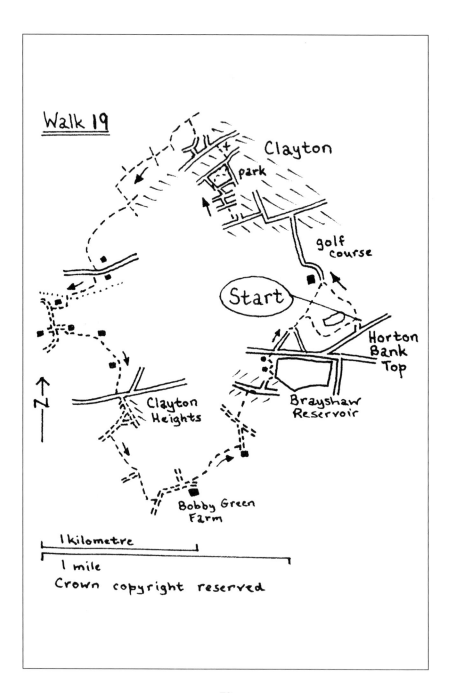

Walk 19

Clayton

park

golf course

Start

Horton Bank Top

Brayshaw Reservoir

Clayton Heights

N ↑

Bobby Green Farm

1 kilometre

1 mile

Crown copyright reserved

Park by a gate on the right. Turn left again (Park Lane). At the T-junction cross straight over and turn right along the footway, and at the safety barrier turn left along a ginnel with Clayton Parish Church on the right. On reaching the next road cross straight over and turn left. Ignore Fieldway on the right, but turn right along Delph Crescent. At the fork keep right, and pass through a stile onto a Recreation Ground. Walk straight forward across this, and on nearing the far side, bear left to leave it and join a track.

Turn left along the track, with a nice view across the valley of Pinch Beck to Thornton. When you soon join a better track, keep on along it. About 20 yards before the first house fork right off the track through a stile and cross the top side of the field to the stile opposite, then continue with the wall on your left to the next stile. Turn right along the walled track, which in 15 yards turns left again. When faced by a gate with a stile beside it, go through, here joining the Brontë Way, and bear left, keeping the wall on your left. When faced by another stile ahead, ignore it, turn left through the stile in the corner of the field, and now follow the wall on your right.

Go through the stile in the next corner and immediately turn right through another stile, here leaving the Brontë Way again. The clear path first bears right, but soon goes left across the field. On the far side go through the stile and follow the contouring path with a steep drop to the right. Cross a stile into an old quarry and keep forward to join a track. About 30 yards before a gate across the track fork right down some steps, which lead to a minor road. Turn right for 30 yards, then cross the stile by a gate on the left (opposite the entrance to Fox Brow) and walk down the left hand edge of the field to the next stile, then turn right, now with the wall on your right.

The path bears left with the wall to the bottom corner of the field. Cross the stile and follow the wall on your left, parallel to the old railway track. (Developments now in progress will lead to the disappearance both of the railway track and the bridge: look out for waymarks.) Cross this by a bridge, then a stile, and bear slightly right up the next field to the fence/hedge. Turn right (the right of way should keep the fence on the left, but if this way is blocked, cross into the field) go through the gap in the wall ahead and turn left up the farm access road. Pass a farm access road on the right and take the next access track on the left. Pass through a small metal gate on the right of the house, cross the garden to another metal gate, and continue up the right hand side of the next field to a stile. The path now follows the wall on the left, but you may need to move slightly right into the field to find a way.

Go through a gateway in a cross wall, and on reaching the next (derelict) farm bear right uphill. Cross a stile by a gate and follow the wall on your left up to the next houses. Past the houses, but just before a small car park on the right, fork right off the track, in a few yards entering a narrow paved walled lane, which could be overgrown. The view back as you climb is splendid. You pass through two stiles on the way, with a gate on the right between them. Walk along the back of a terrace of houses and through an archway to reach the A647 at Little Moor. Cross over and take the walled lane opposite. When it forks, keep right, another track comes in from the left, keep on until you reach a kissing-gate on the left signposted Nature Trail. Go through and follow the path, which soon bears left and reaches a large open space. You are now in Foster Park.

Turn left along the grassy ride, past the picnic table, soon curving right and descending to the left of the large open space. In the bottom corner fork left off the ride along a narrow path to a stile. Go through this, and the double gate in front, walk forward for a few yards then go through the stile on the right and walk down the left hand edge of the field. Follow the wall on the left to a stile, go through and turn left along the track. On reaching Bobby Green Farm ignore a tarmac road on the left, but a few yards beyond it cross a stile in the wall on the left and bear slightly right across the field to the gap-stile opposite. You are now back briefly on the Brontë Way. Cross the stile and follow the wall on the left to the next stile, bear slightly left over the next field to the next stile, then walk straight forward on a paved path, soon with a small wood on your right. A stile leads to an access road: turn left along it. Another track (Stocks Lane) comes in from the right, and 15 yards further on turn right off the track to follow a wall on your right with a wood beyond. (This path may be diverted through the wood: look out for waymarks.)

Follow the wall until you reach a new housing estate, cross straight over the access road to Westwood Park Clinic and walk forward along the footway. Cross the road on your left and turn right along the footway. At the time of writing the development here is not complete, but it is likely that you will turn left along the second street, which should lead to a walled lane, with Brayshaw Reservoir invisible over the wall ahead. Turn left along the lane. On reaching a track, with a stone built house ahead, bear right along it, and follow it as it curves left, then passes a row of cottages, to reach once more the A647.

Cross the main road and turn right along the footway. Turn left along Lingfield Terrace. At the far end go down a ginnel on the right, turn left at the bottom, the tarmac ends, follow the track to a stile by an old gate and follow the path downhill. A gap-stile on the right gives access once more to Horton Bank Country Park. Either go left for a last look from the viewpoint or go down the steps on the right and follow the path round to the car park.

ROYDS HALL AND JUDY WOODS

WALK 20

3½ miles (5½ km); Pathfinder 691. Old tracks and woodland paths. There are two waymarked walks through Judy Woods, which take their name from Judy North (1790-1870), who lived in a cottage close to Horse Close (or Judy) Bridge.

The walk starts on Station Road, Wyke, at the kissing-gate into Judy Woods (GR 147 268). There is room to park here. Take the 363/365 Bradford-Huddersfield (every 20 minutes) or the 622/632/624/625/626/627 Bradford-Odsal-Wyke (every 10 minutes) bus to the junction of the Huddersfield Road (A641) with Green Lane and Station Road, Wyke, and walk along Station Road to the kissing-gate into Judy Woods on the right. Here there is also an information board.

Go through the kissing-gate and take the broad path into the woods, after 50 yards ignoring a path forking left and dropping steeply. At a T-junction turn right uphill, soon leaving the woods by a stile. Follow the path straight up the large field, and at the top turn left along the track and pass through the stile by the gate into an old walled lane. Pass through the stile by the next gate and turn right up the tarmac lane. Pass the fine High Fernley House, and just after the next group of houses on the left, opposite the entrance to High Fernley First School and about 60 yards before the main road, turn left along the unsurfaced Carr House Gate.

After a time you pass Carr House over to the left and the track climbs Delf Hill. When the track turns left to pass through a wide gateway, keep straight ahead on a narrower path (which can be muddy). It becomes a track, which turns left by a telephone transmitter. Follow the track to a T-junction and turn right. Opposite a gate in the wall on the left a stile in the fence on the right gives access to a footpath to Park Dam, the reservoir visible below, to which a detour can be made if so desired. The walk continues along the track to Royds Hall, a fine old house of which unfortunately only the gables are visible.

Follow the track between the buildings and at the far end turn right for a few yards, then cross the stile on the left. Aim about 40 yards left of the large pylon and cross the field to a stile in the wall on the far side. Now follow a wall on your right to North Brow Wood. The path keeps along the top edge of the wood, then drops gently through it towards a garden fence. On reaching a cross track turn left, to re-enter Judy Woods by a kissing-gate beside a gate. Follow the broad path through the woods, with a steep drop to the right.

Keeping always parallel to the valley on the right, the path comes close to the left hand edge of the wood and you will pass a pylon in a field on the left. Just after this the path forks, the left branch continuing to descend gently, before dropping steeply by a stepped path to Royds Hall Beck, the right branch dropping steeply towards the beck, then bearing left to follow the beck down. There are many paths, but keep the general direction down parallel to the valley on the right and you won't go wrong. Both paths meet up at a point where you must cross a side beck by a sleeper bridge. Follow the fence on your left to Horse Close (or Judy) Bridge.

Don't cross it, but turn left up the track, in a few yards joining a footpath to the right of the track. At the top of the slope, with a metal fence on the left, turn right. Again there is a choice of paths: either take the path alongside the fence or the broad path straight forward into the woods. If you take the left hand path, you will eventually be encouraged to bear left over a sleeper bridge onto a broad track uphill: resist this temptation, and turn right down the cross path. You join the other path by a signpost. Keep forward (or if you have come down the other path, turn right at the signpost). Follow the path, now with the beck down on your left, to a stile onto Station Road and turn left to return to the start of the walk.

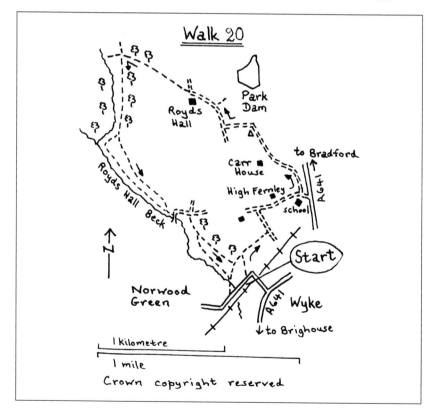

Record of Walks Completed

DATE	WALK	START TIME	FINISH TIME	COMMENTS
	1. A Brontë Walk			
	2. Dean Beck and Keighley Moor			
	3. Silsden to Windgate Nick and the Doubler Stones			
	4. Silsden Moor			
	5. Swastika Stone, Addingham, Dales Way			
	6. Austby and Middleton Woods			
	7. Burley in Wharfedale to Burley Moor			
	8. Over Rombald's Moor to Dick Hudson's			

Record of Walks Completed

DATE	WALK	START TIME	FINISH TIME	COMMENTS				
	9. East and West Morton, Sunny Dale, Micklethwaite							
	10. Around Baildon Moor							
	11. Druid's Altar, St.Ives, Harden and Marley							
	12. Harden Moor and the Worth Way							
	13. Old lanes around Oxenhope							
	14. Thornton Moor							
	15. Wilsden to Hewenden and Wood Nook							
	16. Chellow Dean							

Record of Walks Completed

DATE	WALK	START TIME	FINISH TIME	COMMENTS
	17. Northcliffe Woods, 'Six Days Only', Heaton Woods			
	18. Thornton to Mountain			
	19. Horton Bank, Clayton and Little Moor			
	20. Judy Woods and Royds Hall			

There are four **Tourist Information Centres** in the Bradford Metropolitan District:

Bradford, Central Library, Prince's Way, Bradford BD1 1NN (tel. 01274-753678)

Haworth, 2-4 West Lane, Haworth BD22 8EF (tel. 01535-642329)

Ilkley, Station Road, Ilkley LS29 8HA (tel. 01943-602319)

Saltaire, 2 Victoria Road, Saltaire BD18 3LA (tel. 01274-774993).

Call in to find out about the variety of museums, attractions, farms, railways and scenery which Bradford District offers you. The TIC can help you to get to know what's on on your doorstep or further afield. Each TIC sells a wide range of souvenirs, guidebooks, maps, stamps and postcards and offers an accommodation booking service.

The next time you are passing one, call in and pick up a free copy of the Bradford Metropolitan District Council's Visitors' Guide, which is packed with information about events, attractions, facilities and accommodation.

Here are just a few of the attractions which you ought not to miss.

Bolling Hall, Bowling Hall Road, Bradford BD4 7LP (tel. 01274-723057). A largely 17th-century manor house incorporating a late mediaeval pele tower, with a wing added in the late 18th century. Open Wed, Thu, Fri 11.00-16.00, Sat 10.00-17.00, Sun 12.00-17.00. Admission free.

Bradford Industrial Museum and Horses at Work, Moorside Road, Eccleshill, Bradford BD2 3HP (tel. 01274-631756). An original worsted spinning mill complex built in 1875, now used to recreate life in Bradford at the turn of the century. Mill stables complete with Shire horses, horse bus/tram rides, daily demonstrations, mill owner's house, back to back cottages, café and mill shop. Open all year Tues-Sat 10.00-17.00, Sun 12.00-17.00. Admission free.

Brontë Birthplace, 72-74 Market Street, Thornton, Bradford BD13 3HF (tel. 01274-830849). Birthplace of Charlotte, Branwell, Emily and Anne. Open 1st April to end of September Tues-Sun 12.00-16.00. Admission charge.

Cartwright Hall Art Gallery, Lister Park, Bradford BD9 4NS (tel. 01274-493313). Built in 1904 as an art gallery in the Baroque style. Collections mainly consist of 19th and 20th century British art with a notable collection of international contemporary prints. Also, Transcultural Gallery houses a permanent collection of contemporary South Asian Art.

Includes Indian silver, Muslim calligraphy and textiles. Open all year Tues-Sat 10.00-17.00, Sun 13.00-17.00. Admission free.

National Museum of Photography, Film and Television, Pictureville, Bradford BD1 1NQ (tel. 01274-202030). New and improved galleries include Wired Worlds - Exploring the Digital Frontier, Advertising - the Persuaders' Art, Animation - Brought to Life, the Kodak Gallery, Hands On TV, Tune on ... Tune in, the Research Centre and The Magic Factory - making light work. Open Tues-Sun 10.00-18.00. Admission free.

Brontë Parsonage Museum, Haworth BD22 8DR (tel. 01535-642323). Once home to the Brontë family, today the museum contains period rooms with original furnishings, and displays their personal treasures. Open daily April-September 10.00-17.30, October-March 11.00-17.00, closed for a short period Jan/Feb. Admission charge.

East Riddlesden Hall, Bradford Road, Keighley BD20 5EL (tel. 01535-607075). Rebuilt at the time of the Civil War, this merchant's house has a fine collection of Yorkshire oak furniture, embroidery and plasterwork ceilings. Visit one of the North's finest barns, tranquil walled garden and grass maze. The old Bothy houses a tearoom and shop to which entry is free. Now owned by the National Trust. Open Easter-end October Sun-Wed 12.00-17-00, Sat 13.00-17.00. Admission charge.

Manor House Art Gallery and Museum, Castle Yard, Ilkley LS29 9DT (tel. 01943-600066). Dating from the 15th, 16th and 17th centuries, the Manor House stands on part of the site of the Roman fort of Olicana. Houses local history, Roman remains and an art gallery. Open all year Wed-Sat 11.00-17.00, Sun 13.00-16.00. Admission free.

White Wells Spa Cottage, Ilkley Moor, Ilkley. Built c.1760 as a Spring Water Bath and Well. The bath can be visited and light snacks are available, with tea and coffee made with White Wells spring water. Beautiful setting high on Ilkley Moor about 1/2 mile from centre of Ilkley. Telephone 01943-608035 for details of opening hours. When open, a large flag flies outside.

Cliffe Castle Museum, Spring Gardens Lane, Keighley BD20 6LH (tel. 01535-618230). Built in the 1820/30s and purchased in 1950 for the people of Keighley. A suite of furnished Victorian rooms can be seen on the ground floor. The rest is now a museum of the natural sciences and local history. Open all year Tues-Sat 10.00-17.00, Sun 12.00-17.00. Admission free.

1853 Gallery, Salt's Mill, Victoria Road, Saltaire (tel. 01274-531163). Sir Titus Salt built the "model" village and mill of Saltaire between 1851 and

1876. It is now an award winning conservation area. Permanent exhibition of work by Bradford born artist David Hockney. Open daily 10.00-18.00. Admission free.

St Leonard's Farm Park, Chapel Lane, Esholt BD17 7RB (tel. 01274-598795). A working family dairy farm set in the village of Esholt where "Emmerdale Farm" used to be filmed. Rare breeds, outdoor paddocks and large covered areas. Gift shop and tearoom in 16th-century farmhouse. Open Easter-end of September Tues-Sun 10.00-18.00, October and Jan-Easter weekends only 10.00-16.00. Admission charge.

Keighley & Worth Valley Railway. Operates every Saturday, Sunday and Bank Holiday throughout the year and daily from mid-June to early September. Runs from Keighley via Haworth to Oxenhope. Many themed weekends and special events. Details in leaflet available from TICs. Talking timetable on 01535-647777.

Metro Waterbus service operates in the summer on the Leeds & Liverpool Canal from Shipley to Bingley, stopping at Saltaire. Details from 01274-595914.